THE MOM EGG

9

THE MOM EGG

2011 Vol. 9

Edited by

Marjorie Tesser

Half-Shell Press
New York

The Mom Egg

Half-Shell Press
New York

The Mom Egg, an annual collection of poetry, fiction, creative prose, and art,
publishes work by mothers about everything, and by everyone about mothers and motherhood,
and is engaged in promoting and celebrating the creative force of mother artists,
and in expanding opportunities for mothers, women, and artists.

Editor - Marjorie Tesser

The Mom Egg 2011 Vol. 9 ©Half-Shell Press and Marjorie Tesser, 2011.
All rights reserved.

"Thursday's Kaddish--September 1997" by Peter Seidman is a section from a longer poem, "Accretion,"
originally published in *Beyond Forgetting: Poetry and Prose about Alzheimer's Disease,* Holly Hughes
(ed.), Kent State University Press, Kent OH, copyright © 2009 by The Kent State University Press.
Reprinted with permission.

Cover photo "Walking on Eggs" by Joanne G. Yoshida.
Cover design by Suzanne Altman.

The Mom Egg is a member of the Council of Literary Magazines and Presses.

This publication has been made possible, in part, by a grants program of the New York State Council
on the Arts, a state arts agency, and the Council of Literary Magazines and Presses. *The Mom Egg* is
extremely grateful for this generous support. *The Mom Egg* is also grateful for the assistance of The
Motherhood Foundation.

Founding Editor - Alana Ruben Free
Founding Publisher - Joy Rose & Mamapalooza

ISBN-13: 978-0615464558 (Half-Shell Press)

ISBN-10: 0615464556

Website: www.themomegg.com
Contact: themomegg@gmail.com

Kelli Stevens Kane	(83) 1
Jan Heller Levi	FOUR SONGS 3
A. Kay Emmert	BED MAKING 5
Rosaly DeMaios Roffman	INVENTING A MOTHER 6
Kelly Bargabos	NERVES 7
Lee Schwartz	FROM PRICKLY PEAR TO DESERT SPOON 8
Puma Perl	WHAT'S IN A NAME BUT LETTERS, HUH? 9
Marci Ameluxen	MY MOTHER VISITS FRIDA KAHLO 10
Louisa Howerow	EAVESDROPPING AT THE HOTEL RESTAURANT 11
Rachael Lynn Nevins	THE WORLD OUTSIDE MY BELLY 13
Katie Manning	SIGNS OF LIFE 13
Blueberry Morningsnow	ELIZABETH AND MARY 14
Floyd Cheung	MIRACLE 15
Briony Gylgayton	BOX WITHOUT HINGES 16
Sarah Werthan Buttenwieser	ARRIVAL 17
Janlori Goldman	HOPES UP 19
Marie Gauthier	BABY AT TWILIGHT 20
Marie Gauthier	MATINS 20
Carol Berg	NOW HOT NOW COLD 21
Eliana Osborn	He cries when I leave the room, 22
Judy Swann	PIETÀ 23
Heather Lynne Davis	WORKING MOTHER'S CONFESSION 24
Tammy Bradshaw	LEGACY 26
Nancy Vona	DANIEL AND THE LIONS 27
Nicelle Davis	HOPE IN MY SON'S HANDS 28
Carl Palmer	OUT OF THE KITCHEN 29
Rhonda Woodward	MY DAUGHTER AT TEN 30
Barbara Rockman	SIGHTINGS: SUMMER OF BRAKING FOR BROKEN WINGS 31

Pauletta Hansel   SHOE SHOPPING 32

Carol Dorf   INTO THE WOODS 33

Kristin Laurel   KIDS CAN BE SO MEAN 34

Jann Everard   TRACK MOM 35

Tina Traster   THE SHED 36

Sarah Cavallaro   SELFISH 39

Rosalie Calabrese   A MOTHER'S LAMENT 39

Sandra de Helen   MISSPENT MOTHERHOOD 40

Teresa Pfeifer   TREE 41

Anika Paris   LEAP FROG 43

Caroline A. Le Blanc   GLAZED 44

Donna Katzin   SHIRTWAIST 47

Wendy Levine DeVito   To "A woman with bound feet in a hotel in Shanghai, circa 1900" 48

Patricia Carragon   Mother's Day 50

Suzanne Kamata   PRINCESS 51

Meredith Trede   VESTIGIAL ORGANS 52

Maryanne Hannan   HOLDING STRANGERS' INCONSOLABLE BABIES 53

Olga Abella   LISTENING TO HER SPEAK 54

Ashley M. Nissler   XANTHIPPE IN THE 21ST CENTURY 56

Judith Skillman   WIFERY 57

Carla Carlson   THE BEAST 57

Susan Morse   IN OUR OWN PARTICULAR FAIRY TALE 58

Cheryl Boyce-Taylor   **TOCO 59**

Cheryl Boyce-Taylor   **THE RED BIBLE 60**

Cheryl Boyce-Taylor   BLACK COFFEE AND REMY 61

Cheryl Boyce-Taylor   GOOD TIMES 62

Jonathan Wells   ON MY LIPS 63

Christopher Kulakowski   **MATRICIDE 64**

Heather Haldeman   ON AGING 66

Lydia Suarez   PLACING THE ACCENT 68

Nancy Gerber   MEMENTO 70

Lois Marie Harrod   MARLENE MAE PAINTS HER MOTHER'S NAILS 71

Elsbeth Wofford Tyler   GLASSBLOWER'S EULOGY 72

A. Kay Emmert   ORGAN MOUNTAINS, NEW MEXICO 73

Peter Seidman   THURSDAY'S KADDISH – SEPTEMBER 1997 74

Holly Day   TABLEAU 76

L.B. Williams   SONG 76

Heather Lynne Davis   GHOSTS OF OCTOBER 77

Elsa Mandelbaum   THE BLESSING 78

Chanell Ruth   PHOENIX 79

Kristin Roedell   PRAYER FOR THE MISSING 80

Eleanor Gaffney   This year 81

MRB Chelko   Upstate kids must hang upside down 82

Danielle Taana Smith   LET HIM GROW UP 83

Liane Kupferberg Carter   THE EMPTY NEST 85

Golda Solomon   AN ORDINARY DAY 87

Cheryl Byler Keeler   ALL THINGS WITH WHICH WE DEAL 88

Margo Berdeshevsky   AGAIN, A CRADLE 90

Fay Chiang   BREATH 92

Iris Jamahl Dunkle   GOLD PASSAGE 94

A.M. Baker   CLOCK FACE TATTOO 96

Jennifer Edwards   WOMAN ON THE Q TRAIN, BRIGHTON BEACH BROOKLYN 98

Sharon Campbell   SELF PORTRAIT AS PHOTO ALBUM 99

Claudia Van Gerven   CRONE RECONSIDERS PREGNANCY 100

Christina Thompson   OFF TO COLLEGE 101

Wendy Vardaman   MOTHER CONTEMPLATES THE CREATOR'S REFRIGERATOR 103

Jacqueline Doyle   TELLING RIDDLES 104

Robyn Art   TELLING THE FIRSTBORN 106

Wynne Huddleston   BECOMING 107

Joanne G. Yoshida   Surely people have moments like that 108

Contributors   110

Photographs

Joanne G. Yoshida   Smile 2

Walking on Eggs 109

From "In the Shadows of Motherhood" (a portfolio by Margo Berdeshevsky)

Margo Berdeshevsky   In the shadow of birth 12

In the shadows of a Bali mother 25

In the shadow of the mother's smile 42

In the shadows of motherhood-Belochka 65

In the shadows of motherhood- a passage of hands 75

In the shadows of motherhood-Madeline 89

In the shadow of the mother- a boy's eye view 95

(83)

It's been too long since the last earthquake.
I jump up and down trying to start something.
The glasses in the cabinet clink together like wind chimes.
I can hear them. Nothing breaks.

It's been too long since the last earthquake.
The bed vibrates when a bus goes by.
I jump up and down trying to start something.
The landlord pounds, to say quit it.

My dad called me "the instigator"
because I used to tell my mom on him
for waving to women and eating fast food.
Now I'm on to bigger things.
I am sure I'll be able to do it.

In my dreams, when I jump up and down trying to start something,
buildings leap up into the the sky
and the holes they used to stand in
say AAAAAAAAAH!

Why I can't start something sweet
like a big umbrella over a small child?
Or start something small
like a kiss?

I need to knock something over, so I can start over.
I am strong enough to shake the planet.
And by the time the shaking's over
a song will be left standing.

A song will be left standing.
I am so convinced at the typewriter,
my fingers jumping up and down trying to start something.
It's been too long since the last earthquake.

            The first movement comes.

I jump up and down.

Photo by Joanne G. Yoshida

Jan Heller Levi

FOUR SONGS

i Mother Song

My mother lost herself to the burning flu.
My father loved her, he went too.

World thrumming: loveliness rant
Light shaking on the grass.

My husband wanted children, we had three.
None of them came out of me.
Two grew up, one was born wrong.
Thirty years later, the sickness ate my tongue.

World thrumming: loveliness rant
Light shaking on the grass.

My husband was a healer, but he couldn't heal me.
He buried me under a hickory tree.

ii Daughter Song

The world wears me down with its beating heart.
When it's light outside, I can see the dark.

World thrumming loveliness rant.
Light shaking on the grass.
I've been carrying a slim bone for a long long time.
If it's not yours, I guess it's mine.

When my mother died, I swam a river of grief.
The water wrapped around me like a coddling sheet.
The cold licked my belly, a lampfish my nose,
and ten little creatures married my toes.

iii Wife Song

I met a woman in the park downtown.
She was watching her kids on a merry-go-round.
The five-year-old autistic, the three-year-old, Downs.
Those sweet kids went round and round.

Wear me down, world, with your loveliness rant.
Light keeps breaking on the grass.

You're so brave, I went up and said.
I'm not brave, I just love them, she said.

iv Woman Song

World thrumming loveliness rant.
Light keeps breaking on the grass.

I've been carrying this slim bone for a long time.
Can you tell me what you want of its tenderness?

A. Kay Emmert

BED MAKING

There is no sound but the sound made
by lifting then snapping
like a recording of wings flapping
played back slowly again

and again. Through my fingertips at the ends
I swear I feel sparrow wings
beating halfway between my mother
and me. In my memory

she and the sheet are the same color—sienna.
She and the sheet fall
and rise again, sometimes bringing light.
Sometimes she disappears.

The basin of our open arms reach out
to dip into the pool of the other.
When I fold my corners to hers,
there is no difference between us.

Rosaly DeMaios Roffman

INVENTING A MOTHER

She never lets me
see her back or neck
and her voice allows me
to take the sweetest trips

She lets me change
the names of things
call cars—cows
witches—ugly grandmothers

And she never lets
me know how much pain
she suffered at my birth
how she nearly lost her life

Best of all she teaches me
how to feed the smallest birds

I touch her skin,
it's always just like mine

NERVES

I was fascinated with the cigarette lighter in our station wagon. Push it in and wait for the moment when it popped back out and the orange circle was hot enough to start a fire. It seemed to make sense to use the cigarette lighter rather than try to strike a match while driving with trembling hands. My mother lights up her cigarette and inhales deeply as Karen Carpenter serenades us with her silky voice. "Why do people smoke?" I ask from the backseat of our station wagon. Not in an accusatory, judgmental way that people sometimes ask these type of questions, but in an innocent, curious way that seven year olds ask when they really wonder about things. I had no hidden agenda with my mother and her smoking. This was before children knew they should guilt their parents into quitting because of second hand smoke and the effects on their lungs. I was a thinker and always wanted to know the reason behind everything.

I had a babysitter sitter once, Veronica, Ronny for short, who smacked me hard across the face because I asked her *why* too many times. Then she put me in solitary confinement for the rest of the day. I sat in the middle of an empty room with the door closed for hours.

My mother glanced at me in the rearview mirror as she gave me her one word reply, "Nerves". She said it so matter of fact, like I was supposed to know what it meant. Ahh, *nerves*, I say in wonderment to myself. I had no idea what *nerves* were, but apparently it was something that adults get. It sounded so mysterious, and slightly bad, not something you really wanted but had to deal with, like your period or the IRS. I wondered if nerves were the reason she never smiled or played with us. I wondered at what age I would get them.

FROM PRICKLY PEAR TO DESERT SPOON

Mother was on a train to Arizona September of '43
while they dried the afterbirth from my face
she couldn't breathe, choking on regret,
the smoking car swollen with slicksters didn't seem to bother her.

She had a nimble mind for numbers and was quickly winning
all the wavy haired cowboys' money at cards,
leaving me in a public ashtray at Mount Sinai hospital,
no train rocking to stop my wailing.

My daughter must have heard that train whistle in her bones,
she held on to me like a taffy pull at a county fair,
chewed on my hem 'til it was wet as the counter rag
the black porter used to clean the club car.

What was she looking for in that vast terrain?
that land vulnerable as my own flesh,
Indian ruins and a cowpoke kissing her cheek
exhaling lizard tail inside her wedding ring.

Is it so wrong to want your mother around?
To dig for her in the pockets of your jeans,
search for her hips
as you venture past the gates of the body.

My mother returned east to the opiate of sleep,
I grew myself up,
sliver of sharp bones at the schoolhouse door
in clothes I stretched myself into as the dawn cracked my bed.

You wean yourself from me, daughter,
a lone caboose, our breath and bodies uncoupled,
you lumber off carrying me inside like a lost boot,
all the women you'll ever love.

WHAT'S IN A NAME BUT LETTERS, HUH?

Victor's mother sits on the step.

She holds a poem in the pocket
of her flowered housecoat. On her feet
she wears cloth shoes, covered with rosebuds.

Every day, she waits on the stoop
for Victor; she never picks him up
from school.

Sometimes she stays in bed
past two o'clock and must rush
to wash and put on lipstick.

She did not write the poem in her pocket.
A boy passed it to her in the schoolyard
before anybody knew about her belly.

The boy liked her and asked her name.
She turned away and never answered.
He passed her the note on her last
day of school, before they found out
and sent her away.

"What's in a name but letters, huh?
Tell me your name and I'll tell You
why I like You When I walk you
home we'll eat Ice Cream
in Sugar cones sweet as you."
from Javier xxx

She never went back after
Victor was born. The faded yellow
lined paper is her only keepsake.

Victor is running down the street
with his friends, happy to see her
looking fresh and awake in her
flowered housecoat and her poem
in her pocket.

Someday, she hopes, Victor will smile
at a girl and she will tell him her name
even if it's just a bunch of letters.

Marci Ameluxen

MY MOTHER VISITS FRIDA KAHLO

I *know* you met Frida.

The titles of your paintings reveal it,
journal your honeymoon trip—*Oaxaca,*
Cuernavaca, Tlaquepaque,
Mexico City, 1952, where Frida, unsteady,
greets you at her blue door,

her brows like dark birds.
You hug like sisters, two who enjoy
a dirty joke, burn of good whiskey
whose fingers twitch for cigarettes
and smooth wood paintbrushes.

Frida compliments your accent,
is pleased you can also chat in German
while monkeys watch from canvas leaves.
Diego brings wine in an earthen jug,
a bite to eat? he teases, then Frida

dismisses him – she values time with women.
From a bureau covered with sugared skulls,
feathers, bones, Frida pulls out
her silver hairbrush: you unclip dark
strands gathered at the nape

of your slender neck.
With lean strokes she brushes your hair
murmuring folk songs, love poems,
brushing   brushing
as if you were a canvas
rough yet full
of the skin of life.

Louisa Howerow

EAVESDROPPING AT THE HOTEL RESTAURANT

A boy, head wrapped in bandages,
keeps banging his spoon. I jab at a slice
of pecan pie, but it's his hand

I want impaled. That's when this boy,
no more than eight, says to no one,
to everyone, "I know what you're afraid of,

afraid I'll die." I fumble with my cell,
check for messages that no one's sent,
and again find myself drawn to the boy,

his nothing-out-of-the-ordinary parents.
His father opens his wallet, fans out tickets
like a game of chance. "Great seats, first base."

The mother keeps her eye on her son.
Her son grins at me – "Hey lady,
I'm playing drums" – bangs louder.

She snatches his hands, pulls him
closer. "Remember us in the backyard,
how we played catch." The boy

struggles free, insists it wasn't her,
but Daddy, Daddy. "Tell him it was me,
Harry, tell him." I want to take this woman

in my arms. Yes, yes, it was you,
all of us in fenced backyards,
throwing ball after ball to our sons.

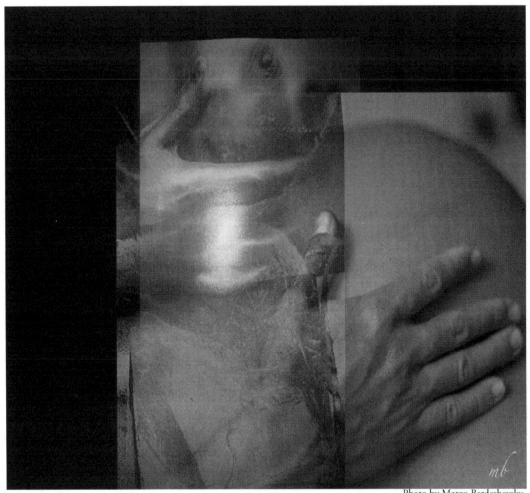

Photo by Margo Berdeshevsky

Rachael Lynn Nevins

THE WORLD OUTSIDE MY BELLY

My sweetheart, this is what life is: waiting for the B23
in the rain. The air is full of the scent of lilacs, and the bus
is late. There will be days in May
as cold and gray as October, and you will forget
to buy milk for your breakfast.
Sweetheart, I tell you, don't go looking for real life
anywhere else
but in the heaps of dirty clothing on the bedroom floor.
The dishes in the sink. The late nights at your desk,
your weary eyes, the moon in the window.

Katie Manning

SIGNS OF LIFE

Little alien planet,
I've got you
surrounded.
I have scanned
your surface
for life and see
you have one
being—bloblike,
almost human.
So, of course,
the question
remains: Do you
come in peace,
or have you
come to tear me
to pieces?

ELIZABETH AND MARY

We are a precision. we are the collision
with other dimensions. and a law of nature and a thunderstorm. rainlines approaching:
with all strings solved into math; the field is acting astonished. but how many inches
of space will be added? what will enlarge and/or loosen? you are ruptured, she said,
ruptured. a star-set fighting its pulse. a moon-zero; demathed moon yet all of its
distances saved as faint rings in coral skeletons. necks dissolve humbly into rain. a
cervix softens, relaxes.   dilated between 7 & 10; nature's
                                        bony rings opening out.
                                        everything not language
                                        is nature, she said;

                                        she visits mary in the country.
                                        the womb of eerie joy jumps. the child
                                        collides with itself;
                                        elizabeth puts her hand there.
                                        in the beginning
                                        there was everything,
                                        she said,

                                        and then
                                        the overwhelming
                                        (humility-
                                        knuckling)
                                        urge to push

MIRACLE
for Annie

Is it still a booty call
if when I get there
he hands me his semen,
I suck it up with a syringe,
squirt it into me,
and lie back for half an hour?

Of course, it wasn't like this
in the beginning. It was almost
romantic, the four of us--
Jon and his partner, Mary and me--
dining over candlelight
to celebrate the miracle of life
and teamwork.

We needed Jon. Jon was kind.
Whenever I ovulated, he produced.
I drove to meet him wherever he was--
work in Boston, vacation in Provincetown.
We were on call for each other.

It became routine, tedious even, but
between giving up and trying something else,
Emma came to be.

In the hospital delivery room,
Mary coached me. Jon had sent flowers.
I was lying on my back,
and all was right with the world.

Briony Gylgayton

BOX WITHOUT HINGES

woman with a white chest big
as a barrel and slick as an oyster
with sweat in the morning by the toilet
I hold my ballooned belly in thick wristed
hands as it swings and sticks and swims

I eat mostly pitted
fruits, crave an inconvenience
as it is winter and apricots are
dry as old women's wombs

I push knobbled fingers against
my temples the tremble thrills
against me and my teeth snap
so hard they float
before day breaks I have not slept once

the falling and hatching
it is at once the only cure
my eyes on different shards of
my belly shell, I see at two angles
the last of me, my
sweet yolk glossed,
sun sopped and gently cooking

ARRIVAL

Caroline, flanked by nurses, one pulling back each leg, was about to give birth. Overhead lights switched on, isolette warming. Hours earlier, she'd received an epidural. "It's pressure," she said, of the head against the cervix, "not pain." Her voice sounded breathy, small, her hospital gown askew, her tangled hair pulled back in a ponytail. Then, almost without warning, her face coalesced upon a determined grunt. She bore down with all her might.

Caroline's sister, Margaret, stood by her side. Caroline and Margaret's mother, Janet, hung back. I stood next to Janet. I'd met Margaret for the first time five hours earlier, arriving at the hospital during that lull after the epidural and before transition. I'd met Janet once before, a few weeks earlier.

Rather than notice the edges of morning light lifting darkness from the sky, the only indication of morning in the labor room: the nurses' changeover at seven.

**

Three strong pushes. The moment the baby's body poured from Caroline's seemed very sudden. It was as if everything changed.

She was the child we were all waiting for. First and foremost, she was Caroline's. Yet, she was slated to be ours, that is my husband's and mine. Somewhere out there Caroline's ex-boyfriend had objected to the notion of strangers raising her, and vowed the baby be his.

**

The nurse did not put her on Caroline's belly nor did they hand her to anyone else. Time seemed to be suspended. Intention seemed to be suspended. The nurse, in full possession of the baby, carried her to the lit-up isolette.

While the nurse examined the baby, the doctor asked whether any of us—Caroline's mom, her sister or myself—wanted to cut the cord. The idea of my coming between Caroline and the baby to sever their shared physical tether felt exactly wrong to me. Margaret and Janet also declined.

I looked at Caroline, who was crying. I wondered how hearing that raspy little voice felt, whether hearing her baby call out might change her course. I'd had three babies emerge from my body and land straight upon my belly to be pulled into my arms. I couldn't imagine wanting anything else at that very moment. At once, I wondered about Caroline's reaction selfishly and out of curiosity. I felt simultaneously wholly invested *and* at a tiny, self-protective remove. I swayed from foot to foot, breath held in.

Caroline had to birth the placenta. Caroline didn't turn toward the baby. "I can't see without my glasses," she explained. She focused on the last bit of pushing. Margaret was crying, and her mother's eyes were damp. I offered a quick embrace, mumbled, *Congratulations.* I didn't want to look at them, didn't want to intrude. My arms wrapped across my body, I was dry-eyed, barely breathing.

I wandered toward the isolette while Caroline's mother and sister talked to Caroline. The baby girl was petite and extremely pink with a full head of damp, jet-black hair. She looked so perfect, with her delicate, almost translucent fingers, long toes, dark eyes, somewhat wide nose, and churlish mouth. She was beautiful.

Had I been mere observer, I might have grabbed my camera; for that matter, I'd probably have already had it in hand. Had I been sure I was the mama, I'd have reached in to touch her, but that felt presumptuous. I didn't want to overstep any boundaries, fearing the nurses' reactions. It wasn't clear what the nurses thought. Apparently, they hadn't been fully prepared for what one nurse called *this situation.* They'd eyed us all warily in the thin darkness in the middle of the night. Had I been certain Caroline was the mama, I'd have begun to describe the baby to Caroline, so she could imagine her newborn.

Janet wandered over. "She's tiny," Janet marveled. I nodded. We admired her granddaughter and my would-be daughter side-by-side.

When the nurse finally lifted up the swaddled baby, I indicated that her grandma should hold her first. At least, I think this is what happened. There is a blur factor here. In short order after the nurses handed her off, her grandmother held her, I held her—minute feathery wisp not six pounds, almost like a doll—and so did her aunt, who gazed through tears that made her dark eyes turn slick as polished stones. Caroline didn't want to touch her until the placenta was out and her glasses were on, but she did say, "Saskia," the name we'd chosen. I exhaled.

Janlori Goldman

HOPES UP

Hard shrieks, a geshrei, a bang-
        busting of delicate spine. The crank-
                handle yanks through another turn. My creaky
                        bones push. The room breathes in
                                yeast, out steam – all the walls
                                    a chamois sponge.

Gut-strained from pushing you nine hours
into eager air, I lift my head
to hear your cry. Trapped
in the tunnel, you're too full of poison
to make it to the exit. You drew in
                                meconium on the final stroke,
                                        sucked into your lungs that first expul-
sion.

Grey and still.
Tar jams every port.
            The doctor says, *don't get your*
    hopes up.

Hopes up is all
I am. All I've been
for 40 weeks, waiting to smack
                the bell at the top of the pole.

BABY AT TWILIGHT

He's a howler, shell-
shucked and new-born, his cry
as round as the moon.

The first stars of midsummer
bank their fires.

Mouth brushing his ear,
your shush meant
to shunt him toward sleep

churns in his cochlear labyrinth—

rain-swollen river-
surge, fusillade and furor
lathering against the rocks.

MATINS

A heavy wreath of fatigue
rings her head—the baby
has foresworn sleep,

barely knitting one hour
to another—the days
smear together like old

bruises smudging skin.
It's 4 a.m.—for the moment
all sleep save her.

She rubs the crusted
rinds of her eyes, weighing
the worth of an hour's

rest against the inexorable
violence of being woken—
as if she isn't already

pinioned to the couch,
sleep's hot breath
a luminous psalm.

Carol Berg

NOW HOT NOW COLD

I don't know how to wrap
the corners of your blanket
so your arms stay still
and your tiny fingers
don't poke you in your blue
blue eyes I don't have patience
to stuff you in the stroller
buckle the four safety buckles
pinching my index finger rather
than your skin and stroll you
down Davis Court pointing
out the red birdy birdy birdy
or wait while you turn the word
four over in your mouth
I don't have time to stand
over the flowing water filling
your blue plastic bathtub
feeling the water now hot now
cold sliver my wrist
I don't have time
to wash your onesies
your socks your spitty up
blankets I don't have time
to cheer your first fist
of cheerios to mouth
don't have an hour
to pick up your wooden
alphabet blocks from under
our green couch from under
our bedroom pillows
I don't want to say
say please, how do you
ask, can you please
say please

Eliana Osborn

He cries when I leave the room,
Bangs his head against the floor
No matter how long we've played,
The songs I've sung, rhythms I've clapped.
Pure devastation ensues, as though
We're separating for days not moments.

I wake to chirps not from the trees but crib.
Opening the door, slow and sneaky
I surprise him and am rewarded with
full open mouth, tongue out, gums spread
Bobbing head and full body spasms of bliss.
Into my arms, up in the air,
The sweetness of a sweaty milky neck crevasse.

I threw up for more than thirty weeks,
When I would stand or lie or try to brush my teeth.
Instead of growing just a baby I grew
Thinner, resentful, unsure of all I knew.
A marriage dying daily,
We speak in passing of our son,
the yard, the pool, what bills are due
Nothing more of substance or even sweetness.

I do not want a child, that much is clear
These are the words I cannot say aloud.
Five years and more I yearned for pregnancy
But one child was enough.
Content I readied to move forward,
focus less on someone else's fluids.
That plus sign on a pasty stick,
A hollow sick all through me.
Day by day I lie and cry and can't go on
Yet morning comes and it happens all again.

When he comes, surging into a dim afternoon
he's sweet and small and I don't mind him exactly.
We survive we four living side by side,
I feel nothing except tired to the cerebellum.
The baby, the brother, the dog, the house
Till I stop staring at the popcorn ceiling

Creating silence between my ears unlike
The roaring chaos around me.

Not overnight but steady, pieces of my heart
awake. Laughing in his sleep, toenails growing
each hour, I glimpse this person who I'll know
for all the rest of time.
I won't be able to tell him much about the wait
and his arrival, but to love this child
is a marvel more than enough.

Judy Swann

PIETÀ

I cradle his length in my arms, pietà.
The house is quiet; no radio, TV, man.

Moon's sheen glides through curtains,
its musky fog, fragrant with hyacinth.

He's asleep, his mouth around my nipple,
a suite of quiver sips, a sigh.

Transferred to pillowless mattress
sleep stokes up his pluck and
he heralds morning with his cry.

WORKING MOTHER'S CONFESSION

Sometimes, in the quiet before sleep,
my whole being tries to become a message,
to speak gratitude, like a little sun.
It just happens, this song going out
to whatever receives us, whatever enables life
to pass through our bodies and land, plop,
beside us, right here, where we dream. This is
my child's unfettered laughter, her wild
animal movements, her mind
open as a field in early spring.
It still confounds me—her hand
pulling us into moments
we could inhabit forever, that have
no future, no past, that require only
a floor to play on. I understand now
that this is living
like a tree lives, without appetite
or ambition, but still growing, connected
above and below, to earth, to sky, stretching
between them. In the mornings, when I leave,
my daughter, four years old, always says
the same thing—*bring me any treat, call me,*
remember everything, remember
everything I told you.

Photo by Margo Berdeshevsky

Tammy Bradshaw

LEGACY

I'm expecting that you'll arrive
with a map of the world
painted on your tiny chest
and spitting out words like Bob Dylan.

I'm expecting you
to put your toes in the dirt
and let the music of this earth
run through them.

You don't have to know
that there are needles
and demons
and fists
and regret
tangled in the corners of your body
waiting to shadowbox with you.

But you are better than that blood
so when it shows itself
I hope you will pick up a book
or a pen
or an upright bass,

and sing to the universe
about the things
you were supposed to inherit.

Nancy Vona

DANIEL AND THE LIONS

We went to Target, looking for Bob the Builder's tools,
came back with a lion costume.
This gentle boy, who dislikes crowds,
wants to be held during music class,
and weeps when I leave him,
is delighted with the lion.

He presses the recording of the savage lion's roar,
giggles again and again, strokes the mane,
pokes his fingers in the lion's mouth.

I want him to be a lion,
someone who is fearless, dances on his own two feet,
reclaims toys from pushy toddlers,
plunges into new situations without a care.
But he is a boat already crafted,
and I cannot change what he is,
only guide him through the water,
make his journey a little easier.

So we listen to the lion
and I wish him courage
and his own quiet strength.

HOPE IN MY SON'S HANDS

A vinegaroon hatches a thousand copies of
itself to devour its birthing body. Life begins

as suckle—mother bled dry. This is what my
two-year old brings me in his palm. His hands

are like his father's—proportioned larger than
the rest of his body, as if born to be a church

statue. The saints are carved to highlight tools
of creation from the great heights of Cathedral

walls. Marble hands are angled to reflect light
from stained glass windows—an effort to grasp

color. This is how the translucent bodies of baby
vinagaroons shine in my son's hands. They are

all poisonous, but shy to bite. My son shows me
how he can balance life and death in his fingers—

how he intuits not to crush the delicate bodies of
this new generation, while the old is eaten alive.

Carl Palmer

OUT OF THE KITCHEN

Expressing my desire to learn how to throw a wicked curve ball Mom says without hesitation, "You'll just have to wait until the baby bottles finish boiling. If you're in such a big hurry you can help by taking them from the kettle." She hands me the tongs, "Put them on the counter to dry while I get Dori from her rocker and dressed to go outside."

The little league coach, Mr. Temple, praises my winning performance, says I'm his new star pitcher. "What a great curve ball, Ace. I bet your dad is really proud."

game ball
placed atop
folded American flag

Rhonda Woodward

MY DAUGHTER AT TEN

Lindsay, long-legged,
prances down the steps, pauses
for a kiss, shifts
the weight of her backpack,
and then, she's off
down the lawn
where grass grows
lush near the edge of the woods
moving through the shadows of trees
leaping over fallen limbs
dodging stumps and rocks
running toward the bus,
running.

In a long strand of fall light,
her ponytail catches
the morning sun, brightens,
shimmers,
then –
the last leap,
the flick of the white tail—
she is gone.

Barbara Rockman

SIGHTINGS: SUMMER OF BRAKING FOR BROKEN WINGS

Did the bloated wren, claws curled to its breast,
attest to fate or ingested bait I'd spread
for grasshoppers? Every sign pointing
to my instinct to kill.

Even jays who'd drilled for berries at my screen,
mistook glass for sky, collapsed
into the ice plant– blue feathers
I pulled like loose threads.

In a boulder's curve, a calliope.
Its humming heart frozen,
whirred wings shiverless.

At dusk, a finch struck my headlight,
fell to asphalt. I thought vet, shelter,
and drove on.

Through rush hour's crush, my daughter
willed a stunned pigeon, *Fly!*
Later, her thrilled song
from our flat roof

until I screamed, *Off!*
My girl's flapping arms
fell, sullen, to her sides.
And I stand convicted.

SHOE SHOPPING

She has come back from camp
a vegan and now we must
buy Birkenstocks, though she still teeters—
Will people think they're ugly, she asks,
as if I might know.

Last year it was spike heels
to match the wrong prom dress
I'd helped her choose: missing the mark
of *almost like the other girls', but different.*
I cannot help

but think about another pair
of slippers now, though I'm the wrong mother
for such gifts in that story, too, step-
ping beside her in my sturdy shoes,
neither the earthly one nor the divine.

Carol Dorf

INTO THE WOODS

In the Armoire there are stacks of shrouds in preparation for multiple demises. Who knew they needed a pattern? I prefer the box of scraps or the jewelry box. Hearing my earring, or is that an errand. We'll lose sounds and sense, we'll find the wrong home. An elegy for a lost childhood, mine; and one that is too close to ending, my daughter's. She's thirteen, and although I keep asking "who is that girl," she is settling into herself. Who is the baker and who is the baked? The girl wants to be the baker and survive the play, but alas, she is the wicked stepmother, always nasty, always in the background. What good comes of the fractured morning where someone is yelling at the garbage man; and then a transvestite wielding scissors charges onto campus, "You stole my book." On the journey it grows dark and we are relieved, almost time for bed, and is there a reason to be afraid of the night?

KIDS CAN BE SO MEAN

My daughter cries but doesn't know why she cries, or
gets pimples on her face, menstrual cramps, asks: "when will this all go away? "

My youngest son, with his round face, and thick glasses is an "easy target" the
        counselor says.
Some boy on the bus said: "go home and kill yourself, nobody likes you."

I got picked on for being a tomboy, wearing jeans with patched up knees;
I was shoved into the lockers and swatted at by a swarm of girls.

It's the boy that stutters, the kid that wears his favorite shirt for three days, bothered
        about the deer
that was shot, its head hanging on the living room wall who is told, "you're so gay;"

or the kid that's snickered at when he has to stand up in class, or the one that jokes to get
        acceptance,
takes risks, cries over papers to get in the best school, chugs down the beer to cheers,
        places the finger

down the throat to stay thin; the little girl with dandruff, shunned by the entire seventh
        grade "stay away
from her, she's got lice," or the shy girl in the locker room, unsure about the hair growing

under her arms, the budding breasts, the world telling her to --grow up --grow up
        --but only like the rest of
us; my eleven year old son almost cried when a fish swallowed a hook, but his friend said:

"Dude, it's only a Sunny, lets put Blackcats in its gills and blow it up."
I'm glad those days are over. Sensitivity is for suckers. But the truth is, I still care, just
        last week

I worried for the large woman who squeezed into the airline seat, overflowing into
        the armrest.
I was glad she fit, and thankful, yes, very thankful as I thought: "at least I'm not that fat."

Jann Everard

TRACK MOM

That's my kid—the one who just dumped his sports bag at my feet. The one putting on his running spikes for the final pre-race warm-up. Did you hear what he said to me? He said, Don't make me look like a tool.

Last night you wouldn't believe it was the same kid. He was hanging around the kitchen looking gangly and nervous. I can't do it, he said. I feel sick, he said. I told him to just get out there on the track and run, the same way he's done five, six times a week for the past four years. You've trained for this, I told him. You'd hate yourself tomorrow if you quit now. Stop whining.

Yeah, I know the sport psychologists wouldn't agree. But I'm not into that "do your best, you're only competing against yourself" stuff. The kid's fast. He can win.

And this is his ticket, you know. A way to get a scholarship. To get out from under this town's dark shadow. He hasn't had it easy. I've made tracks of my own.

Today he really needs to win.

I know I should leave him alone but I have to ask. Have you had enough to drink? Did you double check your laces? He's a teenager after all. I read somewhere that it's not their hormones that make them stupid; it's their brains. Scientists have figured it all out using MRIs. Something about the synapses needing to be pruned before kids can make the right decisions. My therapist tells me teens lack executive function skills. From what I can tell, that's just a nice way to say they're unreliable.

See him? He's waving me into the stands. And when he rolls his eyes—that means I'm not supposed to yell like the other parents.

He's a good kid, really. He always leads his teammates through the last dynamic stretches and a few sprints before the race. He looks loose, don't you think? And those shorts and singlet don't hide the muscle.

I remember when I realized he could run. He was only eight. We'd been driving through a park, looking for a numbered campsite, when he noticed a wasp buzzing against the back window. He screeched in my ear and clawed at the locked door handle before I'd even stopped the car. I was tired and cranky. I braked hard and stretched an arm over the driver's seat. I lost it, you know. It wasn't my finest parenting moment. Get out, I yelled. Just follow the car until we get there.

I told him he'd better keep up. Or else. Why do we say stuff like that to our kids?

Then I drove away. I was going pretty slow, but for twenty minutes he did keep up, running behind the car, arms pumping, stride lengthening.

I'll be damned, I thought.

Wait. Did you just hear the announcer call the runners to the starting blocks?

Funny. After years of training it all comes down to a burst of speed that will last less than a minute.

Damn. Something's wrong. He's too jittery. He's lost his focus. See that? He's scratching his arm, squeezing his hands. He needs to pull it together.

Excuse me. I need to get to the front of the stands. The official is about to fire the starting pistol. If I can just get to the railing. If I can just get in line with his position on the track. Ready, set...see the slight tension of the trigger finger on the starting pistol. He's about to pull...

I have to yell...

WASP!

Tina Traster

THE SHED

These boys are not from here. Slicked backed hair, body-hugging polyester pants, gold medallions nestled on their exposed, chiseled hairy chests, John Travolta struts. These are the boys I met in Bensonhurst at a disco. I didn't think they'd come to my backyard party when I handed them a note scribbled with my address.

They emerge from a low-slung black sports car. I'm standing in a cloud of cologne, introducing them to Canarsie High School's Class of 1979. My dad's eyes narrow. These boys are not from here. They are older. Much older. Maybe 21 or 23. They are working boys and they are great dancers too. The one with the cherry-blond hair looks like Robert Redford, only the Italian version. I hope they will not be bored with us. I fiddle with my halter.

"There's beer, too," I say.

Two of them move through the crowd.

The cherry-blond hangs back. He tells me his name again and asks me mine. "This is a nice house you have here," he says. "Thanks." I'm at ease with boys my age, boys from Canarsie. This feels different.

"So which one of these boys is your boyfriend?" he asks, gesturing with his chin. I giggle. "Oh these boys are just friends." "I see." He stares hard at me for a second.

"Come here," he says, hooking his hand around my waist, planting it in the small of my back. I arch like a gymnast. "I ain't gonna bite you." He draws me in. I glance around to see where my parents are. The night air is thick with damp heat.

The sky is scarcely lit by a crescent moon but I see his blue eyes. I feel his hot breath.

We walk through the backyard past my friends. They look blurry. Like soft ballerinas in a Degas painting. We keep moving. Moving toward a quiet place by the side of my house where there is a shed. He says things I don't hear. I feel like blood will wash from my ears. I keep moving, moving toward that shed. Moving deliberately toward darkness and danger. Unable to stop because a part of me doesn't want to be stopped.

"Come on," he whispers, close to my ear. "Let's go in here where we can be alone.

"In there? In the shed?"

"Yeah," he says, tugging my hand. "I want you all to myself."

I slip into the velvet-black shed filled with summer things and girl-hood. My bicycle. Beach pails. Rusty skates. He is kissing me. The moon-lit streak of light narrows as he pulls the door shut. I want to run. I want to stay. He is kissing me. I kiss back. The shed feels like its spinning. His hands are moving down my body. They are cupped around my buttocks. They move up and under my shirt. I pull away but he grips me hard. Fear mixes with delight. I'm on a scary carnival ride. I want to scream 'let me off of this thing' when I know it's impossible. He says nice things about my body. I like it. He tells me I smell good. He threads his hands through my long hair. Then he takes my hand, runs it down his torso and squeezes it into his unzipped pants. He eases my hand onto his hard penis and keeps it cupped over mine, showing me what to do. He is groaning. I must be doing something right. He releases his hand and says "keep going." When I do, my hand fills with a sticky liquid. Surprised, I jerk my hand away and run from the shed. I keep my hand balled in a fist until I'm in my house, upstairs in the bathroom, washing it in the pink sink again and again. I can't wash it away.

I jiggle the bathroom handle to make sure the door is locked. I can't look in the mirror. I want to cry but I can't. When I return to the party, I ask Lisa if she's seen the Bensonhurst boys. They have left.

Suddenly I hear a full-throated mewl from inside the house. It sounds like my mother. I dash inside and run upstairs. My grandmother, sister and father are rifling through a set of drawers in my parents' bedroom. Clothes are strewn on the floor. My mother's face is smeared with black mascara. "It's gone," my mother wails. "It's all gone."

"What's going on?" I ask. My father stares hard at me.

"Someone stole your mother's jewelry."

"What?" I gasp. "Who would do that?"

"I don't know. I guess one of your friends came in from the backyard and snuck up here…."

"No Tony," my mother says, in between phlegmy gasps. "I can't imagine it was any of Tina's high school friends. I bet it was those boys you invited. The ones I didn't recognize."

"What boys?" My words surprise me.

"You know, those boys who looked rough, those Italian boys. Who were they?"

"A bunch of us went to a disco last weekend. We met them and I invited them, thinking…"

"I bet it was them. I knew they were bad news the minute I laid my eyes on them."

My heart feels likes it's collapsing in my chest. I work hard to push out breath. For 17 years, I've been the good girl, my mother's delight. Even when I didn't make cheerleading squad she found reasons that had nothing to do with my imperfect splits or jumps. "You're my best friend," she always says. I can't tell my best friend what happened tonight.

An hour later, the police arrive. My parents tell the pair of officers how the bedroom was ransacked and jewelry was taken.

"Anything else stolen?" one officer asks.

"I don't think so," my mother says.

"So you say you think it may have been three boys from Bensonhurst?" he continues. "I don't know," she says.

Then the officer turns to me and with eyes like a hungry cat he asks me how I knew these boys. I look over at my mother and father as though I were a six year old needing a prompt before answering a question. "I, we, a bunch of us, last weekend, we met them at a disco." "Then what happened?" he asks. "I invited them to the party." "Do you know their names or where they live?" "No, I say," telling half-truths. "Where was the disco?" he asks. "I don't remember," I say, lying. My mother throws me an eyebrow-arched glance. I look away..

Sarah Cavallaro

SELFISH

My son's friends stay for a few nights at my loft. I hear them piss and shit and take
showers in my one bathroom.
The thought of their bodily sleep washing into where I take my nightly bath makes
me wonder why I invited them here in the first place.
But then I know I'll do anything to please my son even at the risk of getting a vaginal
infection. Scour the tub I tell him.
I end up doing it
he looks at me with a crooked smile
his disdain makes me
take antibiotics.

Rosalie Calabrese

A MOTHER'S LAMENT

Here, now, a chance to tell you
the measure of my love,
describe the gardens of my heart
where you are every flower,
but all I do is ask how things are going,
as if we'd met just recently
at a crowded party,
and it's only your smile that I recall.

MISSPENT MOTHERHOOD

i squandered my motherhood
mistaking it for my youth
believing that because i
was sixteen or twenty or
thirty i was entitled to
indulge in the activities of
youth.
scholarship, art, drinking,
unbridled sex.
dragging my children along
as if they were accessories
like pocketbooks
instead of easily bruised fruit
to be guarded from danger
tended like gardens
raised to be guardians
of the future
of their own futures

i rushed into adulthood
as if it were the answer
instead of the quest.
and therefore i lost
my opportunity to grow
into being grown
up – until my own
children were nearly
grown themselves.
they grew like weeds – no
nurturing, no watering.
they are not weeds.
my children are
wildflowers.
i am their mother
however nonchalant
i may have been.

Teresa Pfeifer

TREE

When her child had grown into a hearty sapling in the front yard,
the mother lost all hope for a normal development and instead
searched for a unique ability such as the play group mothers' boasts
of a child at the piano. Before sprouting limbs
and a few small sugar maple leaves, the toddler had delighted
in a few words: Drink. Cup. Dog. Mama. Bottle. Cookie.
"Tree" may have been one of the last words uttered
before the child's sudden and unfortunate transformation.
The mother's loving devotions continued from a wooden chair
that she'd placed at the foot of the young tree.
During the long days, her mind wandered quietly
among the insects, the birds, and clouds.
The seasons passed but still,
even during the hottest days of summer,
when the small leaves curled within themselves,
the mother continued to find small pleasures in her vigil;
for when she looked closely at her child's trunk,
she could decipher the beginnings of what could have been
a cat, a dog, a cup and yes, even something of herself.

Photo by Margo Berdeshevsky

LEAP FROG

My mother, a fair-skinned Puerto Rican told me
she married my father hoping to have exotic children
Her sister Jane told me she always felt like the dark one
I, blonde and blue-eyed, only wanted Jordache jeans
and unlike my older sister, shaved my legs
without my mother's permission to fit in
at the all-girl private school I attended

We third-generationers get the watered down
version of our grandparents' stories
the language barrier widening in time
the evolution of technology carrying us into the future
while the coquí's song fades in the distance

Even though my Spanish is unlearned
my ears understand it
my hips and feet talk back when the Taínos play

I grew up on the beach in Texas with
tropical palm trees and yellow sun escorting me
most of my young life, and I've returned to it
buying a little house in California with honeysuckle
flavored air, longing to run barefoot across the moist grass
and pick loquats from the arms of trees
And still the coquí's song fades in the distance

It only sings in Puerto Rico
where it feels at home
I want to go back to where I've never been
and sing along

Caroline A. Le Blanc

GLAZED

Acadian Foremothers, 17th century

In *Acadie*, we sleep
thirteen in a one room cabin,

winters we store grain,
vegetables in the loft,

summers, the spinning wheel.
Winters it spins

flax and wool into our cloth.
Covers us, our beds of straw.

Tepee style stands
of wood dry

fit for clogs,
or the fire that feeds

our hearth, hot or cold,
if we are to eat.

Winters it takes more
work to stay warm.

We tell our stories,
sing our songs,

dance and rest.
Once growing season starts

we plant and harvest
every bit of light

between darkness.
The little ones help

mind each other
oldest to youngest.

We raise them
in this dream.

Franco-American Mother, 20th century

Three converted rooms.
Brother has what privacy there is.

The old dining room holds
twin beds for daughter and mother.

Meals are in the kitchen,
after days at the job and school.

Evenings are filled with homework,
chocolate and vanilla ice cream,

black and white TV.
Summer days swelter beneath

Grandmere's resentful eye.
Brother and sister wrestle

bored and angry pretzels
sad about life.

Mum yells, punishes,
measures the worst offenses,

the yard stick between our beds
where she cries at night.

The Last Daughter, 21st century

We talk family story.
"Mothers walk through life

asleep on their feet,"
I tell my grown son.

In the studio,
my hands form soft clay.

Dried, it hardens. Too easily
its smoothness breaks,
melts if wet.

Glazed in kiln fires,
bowls hold ice cream
or the tears of the world.

Donna Katzin

SHIRTWAIST

They trade songs of Poland, Germany, and Russia
to the whir and whine of the machines,
fire in their hair,
galaxies in their eyes.

To the whir and whine of the machines
they stitch shirtwaists the latest style,
galaxies in their eyes
eclipsed by clouds of lint and darkness.

They stitch shirtwaists the latest style
between the bolts and bobbins,
eclipsed by clouds of lint and darkness.
Father warned them not to work on Shabbos.

Between the bolts and bobbins
they wheeze and squint, waiting for the bell.
Father warned them not to work on Shabbos
to fill their bellies stuffed with dreams.

They wheeze and squint, waiting for the bell
behind the barricaded doors
to fill their bellies stuffed with dreams,
do not see the spark in the shadows.

Behind the barricaded doors
they do not hear the sirens in the street,
do not see the spark in the shadows
take flight, devour cloth, air.

They do not hear the sirens in the street,
for shrieks and prayers between the flames
take flight, devour cloth, air.
Windows open. They become the wind.

For shrieks and prayers between the flames
they traded songs of Poland, Germany, and Russia.
Windows open. They become the wind,
fire in their hair.

The fire at the Triangle Shirtwaist Factory, on Waverly and Greene Streets in Manhattan, occurred on
Saturday, March 25, 1911.

Wendy Levine DeVito

To "A woman with bound feet in a hotel in Shanghai, circa 1900"
in the NY Times Magazine
October 22, 2010

Did you know when you looked,
doe-eyed and content at the camera
that more than a century later
I would wince at the pain you suffered?
Your face becomes an afterthought.
The backs of your toes,
smashed and glued to your soles,
point at me. They accuse and instruct.

So once again I am unable to
relax during my pedicure,
when an Asian stranger
massages the story of my own feet:
the once-broken toe that cramps up
after my runs; the stubborn nail
that still refuses to grow back
after I dropped a gallon of milk
on it. She winces as she rubs lotion
on that old scar on my heel, seven stitches.

Where was your barefoot summer
of cool sand and wet grass?
How did you anticipate its end
without the shocking acorn's prick?
Where is the thrill of a kiss
that cannot roll all your weight
onto the balls of your feet?
Did you never dance?

Yesterday, my daughter had a tantrum.
Her father threw out a pair
of too-small Mary Janes. She searched
the garbage and fell to the floor,
"I miss them," she cried.
And though we soothed we laughed

to ourselves, This, she thinks, is tragedy.
In a few days I will go to Target
and buy her silver sparkly ballet flats
so she can pretend to be Cinderella.

And today I will wear flip-flops
for my drive to work because
I know I cannot stay in my
half-size-too-small Coach pumps all day.
When I get home you will be there still.
Staring and pointing and mocking
on that glossy, water-stained page,
resting upon my bathroom stool
on which you could never stand.
I will be tired of thinking of you
so I will hide you with an impossible
crossword and pretend that you
and all our centuries of cruelties are gone.

Patricia Carragon

Mother's Day
my eggs sit
in limbo

PRINCESS

The nurse called her name. Christine rose from the vinyl sofa and tried to slink past all of the young women in their maternity smocks without being noticed. It was ridiculous, she knew. They saw her. They noticed. Even if they looked down at their laps – their burgeoning bellies – as she walked by, they'd probably noted her blonde hair and big nose the minute she'd stepped in the door. Maybe that was why her mother-in-law insisted on waiting in the car – so as not to be noticed.

The nurse ushered Christine into a private room, then turned to her with a grin. "I saw you on TV."

"Really?" So much for being anonymous.

"Yes, you were the Princess Diana lookalike, right?" Christine nodded. One of her English conversation students had called the local TV station. During their early morning show, there was a segment on celebrity lookalikes. Christine had been game, but she doubted that anyone would watch. After all, it had been aired at 6AM. Her student had gotten a free tea towel for the referral.

"You do look like her," the nurse went on. "During the engagement, I think." Pre-bulimia Princess Di. Di, before she threw herself down the stairs.

"Um, thank you," Christine said. People had pointed out the resemblance before, but she was never sure of how to respond.

She actually had a few things in common with Diana, besides a physical resemblance. At 19, she'd been a virgin, and later, like Di, she'd taught at a kindergarten, albeit in Japan. But lately she felt a greater affinity with that other princess, Masako.

Masako, a commoner, had married a prince supposedly descended from the gods. In essence, Prince Naruhito had wed a foreigner. Before World War II, the Japanese had considered themselves special, chosen, and invulnerable to defeat, whereas Masako was a mere mortal. And then, of course, Masako was having trouble getting pregnant. She had only one job – to produce an heir – and yet, after seven years of marriage, there was no sign of a baby. The gossip magazines were filled with rumors of IVF, or of problems with the prince. Headlines blared that the princess was suffering from stress. In her youth, Masako had wanted to date baseball players and study abroad, and now everything depended on how she waved her hand.

"Please lower your pants," the nurse said, reminding Christine of why she was there.

"Uh, okay." Christine unzipped her trousers and prepared for the first jab.

VESTIGIAL ORGANS

That baby ache can kick up
at the damnedest times. Joey's young friend
from work sent a birth announcement. Envy,
that's what I felt. They get the blessing
of beginning, a fresh chance
to start a person. I knew years before
they cut out my uterus I didn't want
more kids, but oh I mourned the unborn
and I mourned desire. The doctor never
even warned me I could feel unsexed.
Claire was beautiful. I could hear
people at the nursery windows oohing
at her bow-tied black hair and tawny
skin. Her sweet breath, the softness of her.

Maryanne Hannan

HOLDING STRANGERS' INCONSOLABLE BABIES

Whenever I see an infant, apoplectic with need (the younger, the better), I approach the caretaker: *Here, let me hold your baby. I have the touch.* Not everyone takes me up on the offer, but those that do never regret it. They see their taut little bag of bones offspring deflate on my nondescript chest, while I splay my hot hands like automagic flyweight nylon. X-treme sport for the Great Mother Archetype. Last night I dreamt I was pregnant again but the baby hadn't kicked in months. Panicked, I did the dream-whirl, begging a stethoscoped drifter to listen to my belly. This has to stop. My hysterectomy was eight years ago. I could go the hyena route. Give birth through my clitoris. But where would I put the pre-baby? Zeus stored Athena in his head, until her due date. One whack from his handy son Hephaestus, Zeus' skull cracked and out jumped Athena, armored, all ready to go. But not a baby, and a headache only a god could survive. Back to hyenas, the crazy-laugh wav files I've downloaded, the rip-your-throat videos: I'm trying to crack their code. So far I know, that despite their laugh, hyenas are not amused.

Olga Abella

LISTENING TO HER SPEAK

In my aunt's kitchen
five women are not
talking about *sofrito* or
the best way to peel
platanos or pick
out the best *boniatos*.

Instead they talk about
Raul's blindness, Guillermo's
dent on his head where they
had to take a piece of his brain,
and Jorge's open sores
right before he died.

He took so many Tylenol
that his kidneys, liver
and heart finally stopped.

They look to see if
I am listening.

My mother has told them
about my poems,
how I tell their
secrets to the world,

but I am in the bathroom
pretending

I cannot hear their voices
behind the door while
they boil beans and rice
put *mojo* on *yuca*
and slice onions for the salad.

They don't want me to hear
how that *puta* Jorge married
went to the mall
while he cried in pain.

I shift on the toilet, imagining
Rosa shopping
while he lay suffering,
when slowly
I hear my mother's voice swirl
above the others, resonating
like the pungent smell
of the boiling codfish.

She speaks of how
each night she bows
her head to God
in grief for giving her
daughters who don't
have babies,
how one does not
even like men.

I listen to the other women
stiffen against
my mother's sudden
lament.

Then my aunt
hisses that nothing
compares to what
their brother suffered.

I picture my mother's
face, flushed chin lowered
as she makes the sign
of the cross, insisting
her suffering goes on,
that Jorge is dead.

XANTHIPPE IN THE 21ST CENTURY

X-chromosomes carry battle-ax genes triggered by
a ring around the finger. So you say. So you
negate my thinking. You who whine and complain of missing
the button on your pants as if I'd snipped it off myself.
Hands hang useless. You stand there yelling you'll be late until
I pull yesterday's jeans from the hamper.
"Philosophy doesn't change diapers," I shout as you
pound down the steps, anxious someone might
expropriate your bar stool before your own ass can overlap
its edges. From there you pontificate, gather in
new recruits who declare you wisest, beer bottle oracles
tanked on Delphic fumes.
Hot words condense on glass: questions to
elicit answers. Here I dig through sofa cushions and find
2 strips of bacon from your breakfast but not the
1 button I am searching for. A gym sock, unpaid bills, cat
sick you said you'd clean up and then just flipped
the cushion. Our youngest, Menexenus, cries from his
crib. I shh, shh, shh him, lay him on the changing table.
Eyes on me, he stills as I rub my nose against his
nose, root into the milk of his neck. I tear open diaper
tape, clean his folds. Our oldest, Lamprocles, wakes,
unwinds his covers, leaves his other brother asleep in bed.
Resting his head against my hip, he whispers, "Look."
Your button glints silver in the diaper.

Judith Skillman

Carla Carlson

WIFERY

THE BEAST

As stiffly bound to the other
as our hearth and home,
we find ourselves like Hera
in a den of jealous words
and deeds.

We offer the nag's head
a sunset, a good book,
or a meal of cut glass,
explaining how
water freezes and ice thaws.

We find the days
last longer than the light.
Our chain is like that tool
grinding against metal
across the street,

where a man who lost his wife
begins another project.
We know in our dreams
who it is our partner
wishes to sleep with—

a woman like the weather,
whose hair shakes
out blonde coins
to disturb the darkness,
its leather air.

At dawn
the great beast growls
for my delicate form feigning sleep
then lumbers away, pisses
a waterfall in a still pool.
A roar of phlegm from the deep
caverns inside his hairy chest
after he scrubs his crooked teeth—
his splattered mirror reflects my glare—
a jewel cat stare.
Like a slopping gawp,
jubilant in my wide eyes, he engulfs
me in his beastly arms, and stomps his feet—
wild joy rumbling wet whiskered jaw
scrapes raw my petal skin.

Susan Morse

IN OUR OWN PARTICULAR FAIRY TALE

1. In the kitchen you peel ripe mangoes.
You carve at least a dozen ribbons, scraping
yellow flesh to expose the underlying pulp.
How carefully you strip away the skin. I watch,
knowing that tomorrow you will leave again.

2. Twice each year we drive you to the airport.
You leave either in sweltering humidity or under needles
of ice. Maine doesn't deal its seasonal blows in diminutives.
You are pale as a hung moon, and I turn from your smile
to the safety of our car.

3. Daily phone calls dwindle. You seem to say,
Face the music, fat lady. This kite flies just fine by itself,
or your favorite, *I've already blown this popsicle stand.*
Your leave-takings become waiting –
waiting for you to come, waiting for you to go.

4. No one holds the trump.
We're a family of great pretenders,
carrying on our night-before-you-leave dinners
and Santa cookies long after they were even
a decent lie.

5. Today you keep peeling soft flesh.
I stare at the damn skins, which clutter
our kitchen sink and listen to your casual whistle.
I look anywhere but at the hard set of your face.
I just know bruising will occur.

Cheryl Boyce-Taylor

TOCO

The unfinished house in Toco
my father took me to
the summer I still loved him

walls still unhung
he draped a sheet
so I could change into my swimsuit
his limbs bamboo slim

he made ginger lemonade
sweetened it with ole talk
and fresh orange slices

the unfinished house in Toco
where later I waited for his 1960's
Green Desoto to round the coast

waited for a postcard
the wonder-of-the-world leaf
grew roots in my notebook

I waited for the flared crowing of my father's voice
across water
the reach of his hand
a ruby necklace to be worn.

THE RED BIBLE

You try on your mother's tan and brown shoes
She bought on our trip to Rome
You keep the lime-green ribbon from her suitcase
Her aqua and white suit for Irma
Her red bible with her name in gold for Malik
Her navy-blue linen blazer for Ceni
Will it fit
Her red and white crochet quilt for Deisha
Will she like it
You sort clothing for the Salvation Army
You go back to that pile and take things out
Her crème car coat for Donna
It's the perfect fit
You wear her delicate white Fossil watch
A present from her grandson
You keep her broken glasses
Her nurses cap with the black stripe
You find her nurses pin
Are those diamonds on it
Zinzi offers to put some furniture on Ebay or is it Craig's list
You keep her bras, socks, slippers, flannel nightgowns
You know you will need her to keep warm this winter.

Cheryl Boyce-Taylor

BLACK COFFEE AND REMY

outside the wooden gate
she walk the dew soaked grass to river
calls to neighbors friends

she want mango and sweetie by Ivan parlor
and ah strong strong drink
from that new shoppe on Fredrick street

she buy goods for the trip
cocoa tea pepper sauce current rolls
doubles roast corn and ah wild piece ah fabric
for she mass clothes

the dress maker better finish that before we leave
the woman on the base
tell she come quick

ah boil mauby bark
douse she in kisses
and tell she stay
my spouse of the word

meh face full ah worry
ah throw ah memory in she purse
braid amaryllis and ah rosary in she hair

she like she black coffee and she Remy
she gather she suitcase
it full with satin silk and madras color

ah say don't
she move forward
ah block the door
ah go
stop
she

she move left
me too

de water calls
ah plait shango in she hair
she throw on ah bright carrot colored scarf
butter cowry ring on she finger

wish I could
stop she
wish I
could
wish

In Memory of Rodlyn

Cheryl Boyce-Taylor

GOOD TIMES
for Ceni

last night we were blues music
shadowing good times
afterwards a city cried out

claiming a stone wall
a hibiscus fence   a raffia door
sky dark and brooding with no stars

a sharp stone fell
into the great shoreline that is her body
her obsidian spine
my unbeatable raft

ON MY LIPS

When she kisses me good night
I think of the kisses not given;
unborn children, white paper,
an ocean promenade of possibility.

The kisses unmade make a poem.
Where else do they belong
if not on my lips.

Christopher Kulakowski

MATRICIDE

dear mom,

i thought you died when i was ten,

but realized you were still alive
until i forgot the sound of your voice.

now, you exist only
as an incomplete
memory.

for ten years, i thought
it was alcohol that killed you.
now i know it was
me.

Photo by Margo Berdeshevsky

ON AGING

"The problem," my eighty-two year old mother says, "is that everyone wants to live forever, but nobody wants to get old." "Age is a bitch," she adds. "And, I know that I can't go back."

"Back to what? What do you miss?" I ask.

"Kissing men."

"You were married three times, Mom. Didn't you get enough?"

"Yes, but I'd like to have the option, again. I live like a nun now."

"But, you say that you're happy."

"I am."

"What do you like about your life now?"

"Well, as a widow, it's all about the children, my grandchildren, friends, and anything to do with movies and TV – anything that flickers on the screen."

"What about your health?"

"I dodged the bullet this year at my physical. I got a clean chest x-ray and passed the heart test and I've been smoking since I was seventeen. Amazing."

"The Parkinson's?"

"It's in the early stages and controllable, but I wait." She pauses. "Don't know how it's going to end up."

"Are you scared?"

"Not really. And by the way, what choice do I have?"

"What's the big thing that you've learned over the years?"

"That it's a man's world."

"No, Mom, seriously."

"I am serious."

"Well something else then."

"I don't buy any green bananas." She laughs. "Just kidding."

I wait while she thinks a minute.

She takes her glasses off. "I've travelled the world and learned that you can't put anything off. Tomorrow's not promised, you know."

My mother is wearing a fresh set of false eyelashes. One is slightly lifting near the corner of her left eye.

"So, Mom, how do you feel about not being able to drive anymore?"

My mother sighs and puts her glasses back on. "It's been an adjustment. I have to plan ahead for everything now." She strums her fingers on the glass table.

Her long orange-painted nails make a clicking sound. "But I love my driver, Sharon. She's newly divorced and single." Her eyes light up. "I'm teaching her how to find a man."

"Oh, and it's interesting to look at the scenery," she says as an afterthought. "There's all these buildings that I didn't know were there. I see everything now that I'm in the passenger seat."

I study her, the mother that I've had all these fifty-three years. Her hair is teased. Her t-shirt is sparkly. Her frosted orange lipstick is applied just outside the line of her lips, making her lips look "fuller – more sexy."

There are lots of daily phone calls from Mom to my sister and me – "an annoyance," my oldest son tells me, "that you'd rather have than not."

"So, Mom, any regrets?"

"Yes."

"What?"

Without missing a beat. "That I wasn't in show biz!"

PLACING THE ACCENT

Every family history includes a dog that bit everyone and adored the matriarch. My mother's mutt, a native of Jaruco, Cuba, was named Motika. She was blind in one eye but could see well enough to rip through my grandfather's linen trousers. Motika left him with a scar and a lasting impression that his daughter in law's family (as his wife often reminded) was déclassé.

"Mom, were there chickens running around?" My mother likes to pretend she was raised on a farm.

"A few hens. But we had trees in the yard that grew mangos, avocados, and *naranjas agria*. Your grandfather made wine for the New Year with the sour oranges."

"How about cows?"

"No, but we once raised a pig. We couldn't give it a name because then it would have been a pet. My father traded it for another pig that was roasted for *Noche Buena*."

"Why didn't you just kill the pig you had?"

She looks at me like I'm a dumb city kid, "It was part of the family. We couldn't do that."

"But it was okay to sell it and have somebody else slaughter it?"

"I think I'm losing my memory. I may be getting Alzheimer's."

"Mom, I think you owe me seven hundred dollars. Do you remember that?" This is our standard exchange. Money she can remember just fine. The last time I phoned is not so clear. "Anyway, you can't know you're getting Alzheimer's."

"Really?" she asks cheered. Telling the truth she knows was a spiteful habit I picked up in adolescence.

"Definitely," I lie. "It's like people who think they're going crazy, you can't know it and be crazy." This adds credence to my claim because of the degrees I managed to attach after my name before school began to turn my stomach.

"Did you know that there are salt lakes in Argentina?"

"And gorgeous men," I add. "Travel channel?"

"Yes," she says but after 50 years in the country, she still says the Y like a J. She used to say cheekens but I taught her how to get out the short vowel sound. I have regretted it ever since. She exacted her revenge, when I gave an Anglo pronunciation to a Mexican beer in a Miami restaurant. She called the waiter over so he could participate in my humiliation.

"Why don't we go to Buenos Aires this summer?"

"With what money?"

"Credito," I answer in English. When we toured Spain, my husband and kids added an O to each noun so they could impress my mother with their fluency.

"I am too old to travel." She "punches" the button on the remote. I've told her it's press but she punches the computer too. The one she insisted would be a waste but where she spends nights researching frankincense, and the Dewey Doctrine and the topography of Mongolia and every other topic that's been on PBS, the history, science and discovery channels It's impossible for her to lose it. She's too curious.

"You're not old Mom." She makes that old lady clucking sound.

"How is the king?" Not Elvis. My son and the person she cherishes most though she will swear before all the saints that this is not so.

"Conquering the world." At least somebody got the blind ambition gene. "Any slackers in your family Mom?"

"No and there were none in your father's either."

"You sure I wasn't adopted." A cluck.

"I don't understand why you don't go back to school and become a supervisor."

"Because I'm too seelly. You told me that remember?" I treasure this observation: a relief from the constant reassurance and confidence in my abilities.

"Yes but you're very smart."

"Smart enough to know I don't even want to supervise myself."

"I went to college full time while I worked full time. You have to think about your future," she says still a guidance counselor.

"I am. It involves bare feet and renting a dog with a bandana that can catch a Frisbee on the beach in Southern California."

"California is too far. What about your children? You never lived more than seven blocks away from us."

"I was overly attached and dependent Mom. That's why God made planes."

"God made families not planes." She punches the remote. "You will never be able to leave them," she says knowingly.

Jes. But would they be able to leave me?

MEMENTO

Forgetting imprisons you
An empty, aching chasm

No words bridge this gap.

Who are you?
You don't remember
And memory is our connection.

Who am I?
You named me, your daughter
Now you invent the past:

Three children.
But there were only two,
A girl and a boy.

See the shadows,
puppets dancing. Here
there are no mothers.

Lois Marie Harrod

MARLENE MAE PAINTS HER MOTHER'S NAILS

I went to the mortuary the day before the viewing.
Just me and my emery boards in that cool room,
and Momma covered with a sheet.

The mortician said his manicurist would do it,
but I remembered Aunt Lavinia,
pearl polish smeared on her cuticles.

He said the feet were going to be covered up
by the satin quilt, but Momma believed
you can tell a lady by her feet.

I painted the toes summer indigo
and glued on rhinestones. Stars, Momma,
you can walk on stars forever.

Then the hands, her little hands.
I wish I could have done the mouth.
Then it would not have looked so strange.

Elsbeth Wofford Tyler

GLASSBLOWER'S EULOGY
for A.K.

I long to lift the lid, metal urn
containing your ashes, press my face
into gray space, seek stranded
scent, smoky hair, trace slivers
sharp edges, tooth and femur shard. Alive

you burned bright as hot blown glass
forges lit with blue flame and brilliant
shifted light, your careful hands
a beacon coaxing forth detail, breath
reminder to burn boldly, blur hue, bend
shape before we cool and fade.

A. Kay Emmert

ORGAN MOUNTAINS, NEW MEXICO

I carry my mother there.
I, who knew her in the end,
carry her to her mother.

On the gold mountain untouched by altar
or priest, *La Cueva* opens in silence
for my mother. I carry her there.

Once my heartbeat rose up inside her
and kept time with her. Now
I carry her back to her mother.

So her mother may know her
I sing *Julie.* I sing *fierce elegance.*
This song carries my mother there.

Up bluffs. Up faults. Up waterfalls
where water froths like milk.
This song carries her to her mother.

A beat rises up as around the old fires,
a beat that is in me, but not me.
In small words, I carry my mother.
Song carries her to her mother.

THURSDAY'S KADDISH - SEPTEMBER 1997

The son asked to bear witness:

Your face is yours
Your cheek   cold   smooth
As when   at bedtime
I loved to touch it   velvet.

Now well on your way   migrating
Through fireworks and demons dancing

You are   and always were

A bird.

The sun shown Thursday
The sky sierra blue   deep and clear
A late summer breeze.

Above your pine-cloaked body
A leaf-shadowed tree.   Within

A crow calls.

I smile   you are laughing

Crow Mother

Agent of beginnings and conclusions
Who wing   bob   shuffle

Not just forlornly stand

Chortling commentator to our chilling keen
You caw down to us

Don't grieve
Dance for me.

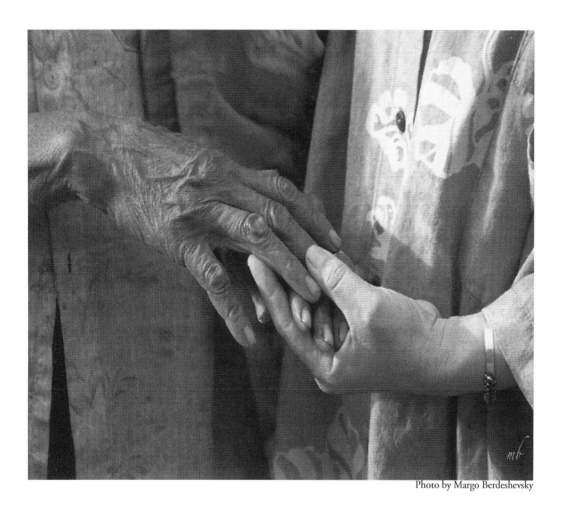

Photo by Margo Berdeshevsky

Holly Day

TABLEAU

when I was six I saw
the stray cat that lived under our house
give birth and kill her kittens
short, spare minutes separating
the two acts. she cried the whole time and I

know where that cat was now
sitting in a waiting room reading
pamphlets about fetal development
adoption options and welfare programs I know
how that cat felt and wish I
would have stayed to comfort her

instead of running away.

L.B. Williams

SONG

When sound is wind
listen to the echo on a road
or the way dew dampens into ground
grief moves this way noiselessly
enters the folds of black dresses
women step slowly as afternoon
bends her hands into oceans of gulls
and sand stoned orange mountains
listen to the way a tree's song
fills the land when the light
from the day is a piccolo
blowing into a childless darkness

Heather Lynne Davis

GHOSTS OF OCTOBER

This fall, it's a song that does it,
collapsing months like a string
of paper dolls who dance and taunt.
Autumn is a death song after all, full
of twilight and wet leaves, ripe
with sorrow. That tune I can't stop
playing calls like a flightless bird. I
adore this season more than anyone should—
its wood smoke ghosts, the sweet blood
of apples, a steely sky, something eternal
in the coolness of the air, even the absurd
color orange and kids tricked out
in rigid dime-store masks. Autumn
is a swansong, holding calmly
the promise of an end, gliding
without effort, always more
beautiful than we remembered—
just like you, my October child, barely
three months grown, then
over in a twinkling, drifted off
soft and clear, gone far beyond
the iridescent mountains—you,
who would have loved
this time of year.

THE BLESSING

"Baruch Atah Hashem Elokeinu Melech HaOlam Dayan HaEmes."

-Hebrew blessing to say upon hearing that someone has died

This is the blessing for the ache in my arms
sore from use: two strong pregnancies
of loss, the year has left me fallow
swollen to hold life
that has fallen away
out of sight, one day

she just stopped kicking, after dancing
on the beach, laughing, writing our names
in the sand, when the evening rose
we sat in the car eating fish and chips
facing the setting sun.

This is the blessing for facing
what makes my heart continue to beat,
it is no will of mine,
it would have faded
to a slow murmur.

This is the blessing for meeting your unborn
child, now born, still and soft
her tiny delicate maroon body

My anchor has come loose

This was the deal I didn't even think
to say aloud, it was that innate:
I breathe, and she breathes.
We continue together.

On a hospital bed,
between my legs, we meet:
I have only seen her

she has only heard me.
I reach to her
to examine the whole of her body
like every other mother in the ward
only I am the one howling
letting go of the world
in an instant.

This is the blessing for mothers
without children,
mothers who find themselves
on the fringe of nights and days,
mothers who light extra candles at sunset,
in the canyon of inutterance.

Chanell Ruth

PHOENIX
for william bennett

I have chosen a strong name for my boy. He will be peanut buttered with
brown, bushy hair like his father and have my eyes. He will be a reader of Illiads
and Odysseys, study Baraka and Barack and grow to love Faulkner's longevity.
Ironically, he will live Hemingway. He will play within the reds and blues of my
heart's garden and steal away my eyes old visions. He will be a blessed child, for
I will swallow anointed oils to insure his gentle birth. Quilt and cradle him in
my dreams of man, of fathers, of brothers. He will be a leader and hold delicate
hands of little brothers and sisters, bridging gaps in the spirits of mothers, lost and
found. I will walk the right of my rib down to a river and testify the joys and pains
of giving him life and killing him, all before he is conceived. I will breathe on his
memory and he will reincarnate himself into white boys who love hip-hop.

PRAYER FOR THE MISSING

On nesting beaches turtle hatchlings
multiply in thousands;
they lie beneath damp sand
until the siren moon lights
their exodus to shore.
Seagulls fly low in flocks
and crabs puncture the seaweed
with their sideways walk.
They wait.

It has never been Nature's intention
that every seed bear fruit.

There have always been crabs and birds.
in another era
Women died of fever beside
newborns on blood soaked sheets,
children died of malnutrition in cold beds
at the back of boarding houses.
Even now there are predators that haunt
antiseptic halls and sterile birthing rooms;
why do my dreams forget this?

I might have lost you
while very young—

And yet to me, you are always
the fierce hatchlings in a thousand
who live thirty terrapin years.
You swim in brackish shallows
with hawksbill and leatherback
diving for waving seagrass,
basking on drifting logs,
and flying through waves
with long thrusts
of flippers.

Eleanor Gaffney

This year

the flock tested winter,
believed feathers, fat,
armor enough.

Their morning lament wakes me.
Snow chilled wings
crack the white sky.

Here in my bed I root
for them to huddle longer,
to find enough audacity

in the meander of their blood
to keen against this loneliness
till thaw.

Upstate kids must hang upside down
in the trees, but the kids in the city I see
seem to dangle, mostly, from
their own minds—limber
little buddies balancing
selves alongside
blackened homeless
toenail deformity, involuntary street
profanity, ceaseless
5th Avenue boobs. Uptown and
downtown. City kids see all the bodies
I never did. At the pool,
sure, I saw bodies
at the pool, but
never like this. I saw nakedness
only under my clothes, so I grew up
slow and stayed
innocent forever. Sure, the kids
around here wear more
clothes than the adults, but their shirts are
are often sad shirts, shirts playing
kids. Clean ones.
Fed ones.
Shirts that match hair-ties and socks.
Shirts free of sex and sweat and disease.
Shirts that don't fall asleep
on the steps of our building, then ask
my husband for a dollar, listen,
forget it, he doesn't have one.

Danielle Taana Smith

LET HIM GROW UP

Sixteen, almost seventeen
In his own eyes already a man
For my maternal instincts, not yet, still becoming
With so much more to learn of life

I worry constantly
How can he survive this hostile world?
I try to teach survival skills I've learned
He does not understand what everybody knows but does not voice
A young black male cannot jog the few blocks home, alone at midnight
In black and white America
That's just the way it is
He explains, he was over at Doug's house, just down the street
You worry too much, he chides and yawns
I did not want to wake you up to come and pick me up
Not knowing that I never sleep until he's home

The police are on high alert at the sighting of a young black male
Someone has called
A boy not knowing he is out of place and out of line, and seemingly on the run
Hands in his pockets, hood over his head, he insists it's cold
Aware of injustice from television shows
He knows and argues for his rights
At sixteen, almost seventeen, he still believes that justice wins
Every single time

There are no witnesses to the night
No explanations to be given
The eyes that peered through curtains
Those who called the police in a panic
Have fallen asleep, resting assured that their lives have been secured

If not the law, then lawlessness is fatal
Stray bullets and victims
Who just happened to be at the wrong place and time
These times and spaces merge
I worry for my son

My anxiety grows more and more an obsession
I panic when the phone rings and when it does not ring
I am helpless
My anxiety suppresses my child, intent on growing up
I cannot let him go
Give him the space he needs to experience life
I am so fearful
I know what happens when a young black boy dares to become a man
I implode with fear and rage
I fight this system, tooth and nails, with nothing left to lose, and life to gain
One young black male to survive being black in white America

THE EMPTY NEST

Last Monday morning, I woke to the cheery sound of bird song. I discovered a bird's nest, nestled on the little ledge outside my bedroom window. It was perfect. Tightly woven, circular, six inches across, perhaps 4 inches high. A symmetrical marvel of avian engineering. A cradle ready to be filled.

Three days later, I discovered one oval egg. An indescribably beautiful blue that made my heart soar. Chicks! I imagined the sight of baby birds with gaping gullets, clamoring and craning in hopeful, hungry need.

I showed the nest to my autistic teenage son Mickey. We planned a project: we would watch the nest every day, take pictures, and keep a journal.

On Friday morning, a plump, brown-gray robin with a warm orange underbelly sat in the nest. She hunkered down low, laboring. Her head twitched, sensing my presence. Barely breathing, I angled the slats of the shutters. Her head cocked to the side, listening. At the click of my camera, she lifted off. In the nest: two, perfect blue eggs.

I uploaded two pictures to Facebook, with the caption, "The Joys of Spring." One, of the mama laying her egg; the other, the nestled egg. All day friends posted comments, charmed by the sweetness of those photos.

Again and again, I returned to the window, captivated by rhythmic bird song that sounded like "cheerily-cheerily-cheerily".

A mother robin can lay only one egg every 24 hours, at mid-morning, because she ovulates only once a day. In between, she fills up on beetle grubs, caterpillars, choke berries and fruit. Her egg comes out soft, almost rubbery, then hardens in the air. She lets it cool so it won't begin incubating too soon. She won't even sit on her nest until she has laid the entire clutch. That way, all her chicks will break out of their shells at roughly the same time. It takes a whole day to be born, because it is such hard work pecking one's way out. Each hatchling has a little rough knob on its beak, to help crack the egg.

Saturday morning: three blue eggs! I snapped another picture. Hours later, I returned to check on them.

The nest was empty.

Distraught, I peered into the garden. "Look at that tree!" my husband cried. On a nearby branch, a black crow sat squawking. Gleeful. Bits of blue shell hung from his beak.

I wanted to kill it.

When my older son Jonathan was small and got sick, I used to say, "let's build a bird's nest." I would cozy the couch with cushions and pillows and his beloved Peter Rabbit quilt and tuck him in. A bird's nest is such a perfect metaphor for security and nurturing we don't even think about it. Mothers-to-be often talk about the overpowering urge to "nest." But for the first time I was struck how it truly is a harbinger of spring. Incipient life.

I shared the sad news on Facebook. "I was so looking forward to your daily updates," my high school friend Linda posted wistfully. *Birds die every day*, I kept telling myself.

It has been a hard week, not merely due to the loss of one little nest. My 17 year old son Mickey is in a life skills class at the local high school, with other developmentally disabled teens. One afternoon, his homework folder contained yet another work sheet. It was an illustration of a bird. He was expected to label the parts.

"This isn't life skills! Why are they wasting time teaching academics like this?" I raged to my husband. "Does he really need to recognize an upper from a lower mandible? Why aren't they focusing on things like how to wait for change when he pays for his lunch sandwich?"

It's a fight we've been waging since ninth grade. We requested a team meeting. The teacher described the challenging behaviors Mickey was having at school the past two weeks. Calling out. Running away. He suggested there might be something medically amiss, even though we haven't seen those behaviors at home. We aren't sure exactly what is worrying our son. But we have a clue. In class last week, a classmate loudly invited three students to his party, and when my son said, "I want to come too," cruelly retorted, "*You're* not invited."

At Thursday's school meeting, they told us our son cannot focus long enough to work anywhere in the real world. "He isn't ready," they said. Isn't that what "life skills" is supposed to be teaching? They used phrases like "sheltered workshops for the disabled." I had the sinking sense that school personnel were just biding time, waiting until my boy is 21 and they can legally discard him. Out of the school nest.

I think about the metaphoric Empty Nest Syndrome. A symbol for parents whose children have left home, and the ensuing sense of loneliness, loss and regret they feel. Many of my friends are just beginning to experience this stage, as their youngest children depart for college. This week, I received an invitation from the high school PTA to a workshop on "helping your child survive freshman year at college away from the safe nest of home."

I will not have an empty nest. My son will live with us for a long, long time, until the day we can't do this any longer. Then we will have to find a safe group home for him. A thought so painful I cannot breathe.

Instead, I am fixated on the bird's nest. "Stop anthropomorphizing," I tell myself sternly. "Nature is arbitrary and cruel."

But here's what I want to know. Where was that mother robin? Why didn't she dive bomb that thieving crow? Why was she so helpless to protect her young?

Why am I?

Golda Solomon

AN ORDINARY DAY

It's a good day
Sun crashing through mortar haze
It's a good morning to shampoo her hair
Pull of comb through tangle
Clean squeak of almost forgotten normalcy
She holds her son
Lets him play peek-a-boo in her damp waves
His laughter and then
Familiar rat-a-tats, repeats
The blast catches them unaware
Both are headless
Her body, strong curves and strong legs
She wears the slings and arrows of unresolved conflict
Her armpits sweat paper-mâché headlines
His libidinal physical response
Remnant of a next generation, gone
Is war a dance of men's erections ?

Cheryl Byler Keeler

ALL THINGS WITH WHICH WE DEAL

1.
Near the church where my mother married fifty years ago, a gunman ties up ten Amish schoolgirls, shoots them *execution–style,* then himself. *I am filled with so much hate,* he writes, nine years after his infant daughter died. The dead father leaves three children and a wife, who he talked with on his cell phone while the schoolgirls listened.

2.
Crows in the meadow where I sit, jet trails above, gnats like anxious mothers. The sun is firm and warm; a breeze massages wildflowers. The Amish families invite the killer's wife to their girls' funerals, say they have *forgiven him.* This quaintness is odd; isn't it *normal* to hate? To fight on in Iraq? An orange moth lights on my notebook.

3.
After five years, our President floats a wreath, purses thin lips. Our enemy is still out there, *hating us,* he says; *I won't forget!* Sun, after days of drizzle. Cicadas insist. So few moments to breathe at work: I dash from phone to filled cart to computer, back to phone. I am turning to vinegar and must be used more sparingly. Jays screech across the meadow.

4.
Fog lingers; air is soft and full of oxygen. I pull blackened marigolds, shake loose dry seeds, bury them in loose coffins of soil. It is mid-October. One neighbor rides his green mower over maple leaves, another hires a realtor, leaves to live with children, a third one takes his mother to the hospital, where she dies. *All things with which we deal,* writes Emerson, *preach to us.*

5.
Predawn in Pennsylvania, bulldozers flatten the schoolhouse where the Amish girls crumpled one by one. Cows will graze where their bodies laid.

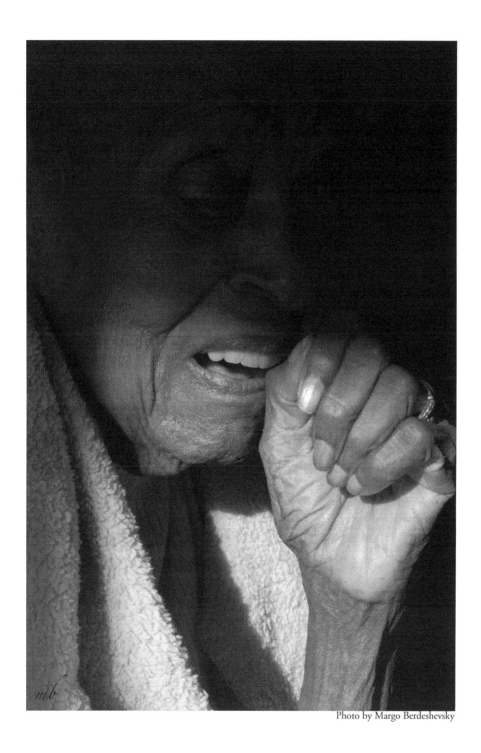

Photo by Margo Berdeshevsky

Margo Berdeshevsky

AGAIN, A CRADLE

i.

Again, the cradle. The bough breaks, the cradle,
quiet while lions wear their war weeds, bury silence,
quiet while a child in stains screams —*everything,*

everything here smells like the gas!
her propeller hands like trapped rabbits, twitching,

my hair,   my mouth,   my breasts   —look!
her tiny fingers try

cracking   the bough,   collapsing   the cradle—
look! my grandmother's bracelets all buried—

Look, no face! Look, it's morning.
Look, it's God.   In Gaza.

Bandwagons line for each abject word —
where wheels don't stop exploded infants' fists,

or mother-skulls, lost,   lost mornings—

Brave holy land war.
Bright. Sun-split.

Where the bough has killed its cradle.

Bright, sun-lit ash,
its inexcusable shroud, rocking.

ii

They swept the dead like loosened crumbs from their fingertips, claws, curled. Brushed
the dust, swallowed handfuls, hungry. Invented noise— in all that silence.

iii

An egg in her tiny right hand, blinded, seraph-child, she — was what was left of what had
finished. Small-winged cataract, not much more. Killed

cradles, and skins, and old men, and kissing — stopped. Egg, in her sweaty small right hand, that hatchling meant for morning. Morning meant for saving. Or yet another prophet.

Prove it.

iv

She stole an egg
from the beast's bed — reeking, heaving nest builder.
Stepped blind, like vengeance. A cinder, empty eyed.
Hovered like a cloud of summer wasps.
Shifted, a gaunt lighthouse onto
promise, across all slaughter.
Reached. — Held it.

What emerged bit her. What cracked its shell
licked her. What emerged, wanted her.

To do it all again.

v.

It didn't happen that way. She held the egg she'd stolen from God's nest and He whispered to her: Good riddance to it and to you. See if you can do any better with this one.

I tried and I'm tired of making eggs. Believe you stole it if that makes you feel brave or dangerous. Blessings. He showed his teeth.

It never—mattered, which came first, the father, or the mother, or the egg. Go ahead, my good thief. Go ahead, my bad angel. Bless. Happy morning.   She held the warm oval.

Held the breaking, mottled, hot ellipse. Couldn't remember —   why. — Breathed it. Waited to feel a nervous thin-skinned thrum. One heartbeat.

She held it for such a long winter.

Hyacinths were blooming in January. Snows froze them, washed them. Still, she held it.

Her eye like the promise she finally remembered —   but from whom? — on a sparrow.

for Gaza. 1/2009

91

Fay Chiang

BREATH

I. Still
      oh heart!

    Still
      oh soul!

    Still
      the mind racing

    Time for accounting:
      what to keep
      what to leave behind

    Moving into one's
      sixth decade
      there's no room for
          bitterness

II. Blessed by
      friends and family and those
      who have brought me
        towards light and air---
            breath---
        in darkened times

     away from those who
        silence and
        diminish

III. Walk cool, glistening streams
        under sun and star-filled skies
        taste rosehips and berries dotting
            beach dunes and
        hear surf pound and roar

     Stand atop and gaze from
        mountain peaks
        graffiti emblazoned
            urban towers

Eyes closed
    bow in calm stillness
        of monastery
    monks chanting to Buddha

mindful of the good
    in this world---
warm voices and laughter
    over meals made and shared together

Celebrate those exploding into this world
        from their mother's womb
            and
        those leaving mother earth for
            a twilit universe
            and
        all points in between

        ever mindful of love and joy
            in this life

IV. Autumn brings again
        its golden light
            gingko leaves drifting
            playfully in the wind and streets
            magenta morning glories
            climb rusty fences here,
            in the East Village

So much undone

and yes,
    so much to do

Iris Jamahl Dunkle

GOLD PASSAGE

for Lola Montez and Lotta Crabtree, 1853

1

In Grass Valley, the child star who tap-danced
on an anvil at Miner's camps was taught
the ancient dance tarantella,
a movement that was once used to trick the body,
bitten by spiders, into health.
Her elder teacher, who wore her age
on her face, granite-edged,
displayed on the stage in her dark salon
how one can shimmy and turn the past
toward the redemptive light
that only birds can see,
what illumes our path forward is what has once consumed us—
a projection answered in showers of gold dust,
more than what can fit in a tiny shoe.

2

Today, we push bowls of alms to the sky. We record scales of our notations.
But we forget we are fragments in ascent—
the thick, black cabled trolley that glides
dangerously close to cliffs confessing
history like lovers in hot punctuated breath.

At the center of the mountain a cool, undiscovered lake resides
chorus of voices whispering beneath water's skin—you are not alone
dangerous, bruised by indecision.

Dive.

Photo by Margo Berdeshevsky

CLOCK FACE TATTOO

There was a broken clock inside Elaine. It once chimed with the hours of grief or joy, even misery. Now she looks at her family with removed and uneasy affection and wonders why the clock does not click, or chime, or move at all.

December: Elaine filled out the boxes of November, the month recently gone. It bothers her to let a month of the wall calendar sit blank when she knows it wasn't an empty month.

pick Roger up from airport

She penciled this in the box of the fifteenth before her husky eleven-year-old son came home from school and said, "I need twenty-four burritos for our Multi-Cultural Celebration tomorrow." He handed her the letter from the teacher, paper stained with ketchup. Elaine saw the date was from a week ago.

"Why do I get this only now?"

"Guess I forgot," Jake says, and he goes to his room. A minute later she hears the explosions of video games rumbling behind his closed door.

*

The burritos failed and Elaine sent Jake to school with a box of pre-baked sugar cookies with red and green sprinkles. She smirked inwardly, thinking of the absurd cliché of *burritos* for a multi-cultural celebration. On her way home, she noticed a small coffee shop and she wanted to step through the door of the cottage-like coffee place before going home to clean toilets and do laundry. In line, she meets a woman with beautiful tattoos. Elaine never thought of tattoos as *beautiful*, but was drawn to the elaborate color worked into the tattoos; she was drawn to the depth of a pyramid that covered the girl's bare neck. It was yellow and dimensional, soft and hard, angled and smooth all at once. The young woman turned to see Elaine staring at her, and Elaine blushed.

"I was admiring your," Elaine said, but couldn't think what to call the tattoo. "Your work," she said.

The girl covered with portraits and landscapes handed Elaine a card and, referencing the name printed in white on the black background, "Tim does awesome work."

*

The card slipped to the bottom of Elaine's panty drawer. Her husband rumbled through the bedroom like most evenings. As he walked down the hallway to the master bath, he left a trail of the day: a tie, a shirt, pants on the bed.

"Oh, yeah, Elaine," he called from the toilet room. "You need to mend those pants. I ripped them today. Guess the gut's growing again."

"In the morning," Elaine said. She pushed her plastic framed glasses onto her nose and returned to her book.

"Got to be now. I mean, you didn't do the laundry today, so I'll have to wear them tomorrow."

But I did do laundry—you keep outgrowing your goddamn pants, she thought. She swallowed the words and let them settle, then let her book fall to the floor. She grabbed a pair of scissors from the nearby sewing box and searched the crotch for the shredded fiber of a small rip. Elaine jammed the blades of the embroidery scissor into the crotch-rip and tore the gray fabric with liberating and happy anger while her husband crapped in the toilet down the hall.

*

January: Elaine sees the black business card with white blocked print and calls the number beneath Tim Hopper's name. She makes the appointment and thinks about what she will ask him to tattoo her with. She decides: a clock. It would be a round clock face with simple hands pointing to the hour three (it seemed a good hour for whatever reason). The clock face would possess depth and shades of gray. She asked Tim, when she met the artist on a Thursday, if he would do this, and he said, "Tell me where?" She thought a moment, and held out her arm: *there*, she said, and pointed to the tender flesh of the underside of her forearm.

The tattoo takes time to press into her flesh, and time to heal. Her son is embarrassed by his mother's tattoo, and her husband is offended. But Elaine loves to look at the circle of time that marks her arm, and somewhere within her the soft and steady tick of the internal clock begins. It chimes, even, ever so slightly and softly, with an hour of self-recognition.

Jennifer Edwards

WOMAN ON THE Q TRAIN, BRIGHTON BEACH BROOKLYN

She writes pornography.
Maybe.

She writes pornographically.
Pen rhythmically
scrawling
committing words to
paper.

Knuckles like knees
forced open
reveal glimpses of
pale skin between
middle and ring fingers.

Plasticized nails
air-brushed tangerine, cream and black,
dig the fleshy shaft
of a blue, roller-ball BIC.

Notebook bends
under her full weight and
with a satisfied half-smile
she presses deeper:
deeper into the page
deeper into her thighs.

She engraves moments
unspoken
into burnable,
spiral-bound
sheets.

Sharon Campbell

SELF PORTRAIT AS PHOTO ALBUM

A tiny blond in mary janes,
pigtails and pink patterned dress
matching mama's, later a good-girl
choir gown and cheerleader skirt,
turned rebel with unkempt hippie hair,
chamois shirt, ripped blue jeans, feet bare,
until, bored being bad, I ordered the new
preppy look, head to toe plaid, from LL Bean.
Because college girls were mean I accessorized
With men: that's me in khakis, binoculars in one hand
And on the other, the safari guide boyfriend
I later traded for a senator's son whose red cashmere
and goofy reindeer necktie suggest a Christmas
photo op. Here I am in knee boots on my mare,
There, a soccer mom, sneakered foot posed
on mottled ball, tiny towhead son hugged close.
Personae mutable as photographers' backdrops,
comfortable as a chameleon on Sunday
funny papers. Painted against Dutch Masters'
black, would anything be revealed
by relentless sunlight on my face?

Claudia Van Gerven

CRONE RECONSIDERS PREGNANCY

It was not a Luvs commercial.
It didn't wear puffed sleeves.

The boy was not yet a boy. He was not a fish
you swallowed either. And those messages

you received were not God playing your ribs
like a flute. There was no instruction book.

The Doctor's smile explained nothing. None
of the booties you knitted touched the ground.

You had no ticket to ride that runaway train.
And the story was not *The Runaway Bunny.*

You were never a rose bush, nor a Madonna
squirting milk like a wine sac. You were not

the Lady of Shallot, drifting limp as a lily
on an antique sea. His rosebud lips

never sucked the fierceness from your bones.
You never gave his loneliness a name.

You had no protocol nor excuse for the enormity
of that invention. None of it will ever be published

in a language you understand. You cannot imagine
the ground you have covered.

OFF TO COLLEGE

A couple of days from now we will all pile into the car — me, my husband, and our three sons — and drive six hours to a college town in upstate New York, where we will deposit our eldest child in a dormitory with his trunk, his laptop, and his borrowed mini fridge. Then we will go out to dinner, and when we all pile back into the car for the return journey, there will be four of us and not five.

Everyone I know with a child going off to college for the first time is in the grip of some pretty strange emotions. On the one hand, they are justifiably proud of their children's achievement and not a little pleased with themselves for having shepherded their offspring to this point. At the same time, it is hard not to be overwhelmed by nostalgia for the little boy or girl who has, quite inexplicably, grown up.

Of course, this feeling of melancholy has another deeper source. As a rite of passage, going off to college signals not only the end of childhood but the end of a parenting phase as well. A clear intimation of mortality, it is a reminder that the arc of our lives is reaching its zenith and we are starting out upon the downward course. This alone would seem to be enough to account for the weird whipsawing of emotions. But there is a still crazier element to all of this, which I, for one, certainly did not expect.

I am not one of those people who has held on tightly to her own college memories. I don't go to reunions; I haven't kept up with old friends; I've visited my college campus perhaps once in thirty years. But this summer my dreams have been filled with familiar cinderblock hallways and large square rooms that, for some reason, I have to share with someone I don't know. Faces I haven't seen in decades swim unbidden into view, while feelings I left far behind me have come surreptitiously sneaking back.

I had intended to spend these past few months researching a major project and my office shelves are filled with volumes on the historical ecology of Pacific Islands and the lexicon of proto-Oceanic. Yet here it is, August, and what have I done? I have spent the entire summer re-reading D. H. Lawrence, a writer I loved in college but one I've long considered unreadable by anyone past the age of twenty-three, and listening over and over to "Fitzcarraldo," The Frames' tribute to Werner Herzog, who, when I was in my early twenties, was widely considered a god.

All this subconscious time travel has no doubt been helped along by the many ways in which I have had to be actively involved in getting my son off to college. I have processed an endless round of forms: loan applications, health insurance waivers, elective tuition refund plans. I've nagged him about his thank you notes and run interference for him with financial aid. And if I've spent a little more time studying the course catalogue than was strictly necessary to help him pick a writing seminar, it wasn't because I somehow imagined these were classes that I was going to take.

I do understand my role in this process and I am not confusing myself with my son. But something somewhere *is* getting confused — and I think it's the person I was thirty years ago with the person I am now.

I always expected this transition to arouse a set of emotions that had to do with the relationship between me and my child. I expected to feel something *as his mother*, some combination of joy and loss. What I did not expect was to have my own subconscious hijacked or to re-inhabit so vividly the person I was all those years ago when I went off to school. For months now I have had the feeling that I was getting ready for something important. Who knew that it would be a dose of déjà vu?

Wendy Vardaman

MOTHER CONTEMPLATES THE CREATOR'S REFRIGERATOR

She's so damned
proud
of them—drawings, songs, the things they say
when they don't know
she's listening: she's got to tell
someone, pulls out the thick fistful
of photos that she carries everywhere. When they see her coming,
the angels and saints start humming,
stare heavenward, try to act
busy, but that's a benefit
of being boss—you get to talk about your kids whenever
and however long you want. Still, she knows better
than anyone:
when they make a sudden
leap—metallurgy, Relativity,
Impressionism—she's unbearable for days—all smiles. Used to be
she hung their projects up where everyone could look,
but the night's blank
wall got so crowded that she had
to stick most of them in boxes to sort later, leaving behind
the early, simple ones she still sighs to remember.
It's so much easier
to believe
in them, in their love,
when she can look over her shoulder
and see those early, spattered, corners-curling offerings there.

Jacqueline Doyle

TELLING RIDDLES
for Tillie Olsen (1912-2007)

"You'll never guess this one." He squirmed in his seat belt and eyed his mother sideways. "Are you listening?"

"I'm listening," she said, half absorbed in traffic. They needed to stop at the supermarket on the way home. She'd forgotten to put eggs on the list. "Eggs, eggs," she thought. "I have to remember eggs."

"I run but I don't have legs. What am I?"

"I don't know, Timmy. What are you?"

"Come on. You have to guess, Mom. What runs without legs?"

"A car?"

"No, no," he said, excited. "I'm a nose!"

"Good one," she said. "How about this. You can't use me unless I'm broken. What am I?"

"Don't tell me. I'm thinking." He closed his eyes, enrapt, then shook his head. "What are you?"

"I'm an egg."

"I have another. I have another. It's not a riddle. It's a question. What comes first, the chicken or the egg?"

"Now that's a hard question, Timmy."

"So how about this one?"

They lay naked on top of the sheets, the sweat drying on their bodies. Sprawled on her stomach, Marcia arched her back as he ran a finger down her spine.

"What is broken as soon as you name it?" she asked.

"I don't know," Jeff said.

"Just guess then. What's broken as soon as you name it?"

"You mean love, like saying 'I love you'?"

"No, I don't mean saying 'I love you.' Do you think that breaks the spell or something? That word 'love'?"

"No. I mean I was just guessing. I don't know," he said. "So what breaks when you name it?"

"Silence."

"Ah, silence."

"I've got another for you." She rolled over and nestled her back into his chest, spooning. "You can't keep it until you give it."

"I give up."

"A promise."

"Are you trying to tell me something?" Jeff asked her.

"No. It's just a riddle."

"Here's a riddle for a fellow senior citizen," Ruth said to Isabel. "It was in the paper this morning. What goes up but doesn't come down?"

"Everything I can think of is succumbing to gravity, not going up. So what is it?"

"Your age."

"Can't argue there," Isabel said. "I've got another gravestone epitaph for you. I can't tell these to my kids. 'You're being morbid again,' my daughter tells me. This is a real one. In Ohio, I think. 'Here lies an atheist. All dressed up and no place to go.'"

"Now that's funny, not morbid," Ruth said. "Kids just don't have a sense of humor."

"Grandma, Grandma, tell me a riddle."

"I know no riddles, child," Eva said as she turned away, hugging her silence close. They wanted so much—her husband, her children, their children.

"I know a riddle. Do you want to hear it?"

"Tell me your riddle, then."

"When you don't know what it is, it's something, but when you know what it is, it's nothing."

Her mind drifted over the past, the curiosity and appetite for life she'd felt in her youth, the dancing girl she'd once been. Was it life, something before you knew what it was? Or death? Nothing when you did?

"Tell me," Eva said. "I don't know."

"It's a riddle! The answer is a riddle! Something when you don't know what it is, but nothing when you do!"

"What is the answer?" they asked Gertrude Stein on her deathbed. "What is the question?" they said she replied.

TELLING THE FIRSTBORN

Like time to a wound it is never enough: the world outside our door,
autumnally-torn and glistening, a muscular November wind driving
the skunk into hiding, the mole to its nunnish abode.
South and west of here, in the yokel towns, the living is cheaper

if not necessarily easier. In some sense everything
has already happened—hair in a comb, a sinkful of crusted knives.
The earth presumably turning and very few falling off.
You will see: life is long, and the body, intractable and wily, going

door to door. Should you incur happiness,
hoard it like a cellarful of winter plums. Should you
incur a man with a list of priors, vamoose.
If in some walleyed previous incarnation we were led to believe

in rust sealant, bloodless surgery, forgiveness,
well, that was then.
Now it's the eponymous swan song
calling the faithful toward their dictaphonic

lives in the exurbs. Like a girl in a Journey song,
be everywhere at once: Love,
a brushfire   over stone, fire
into flame without burning.

Wynne Huddleston

BECOMING

She gave him birth, then left him on the shelf;
he lay there, neither dying nor living
for many years. Then one day she was dusting
and saw him, picked him up in delight,
and said, O*h! I'd forgotten you,*
child! Let me hold you and see what I
can do with you. Are you worthy
of my time? He smiled, filling her
with hope. She kissed his cheek, played
games with him, and nursed him to health,
then asked, W*hat do you want to be*
when you grow up? He said
nothing, so she set him back
on the shelf. The next morning when she
awoke, he came to her and spoke,
I'm all grown up and this
is what I am. She said, *I never dreamed…*
then searched his face and nodded, *of course!*

Surely people have moments like that

You're riding down the main beach drag, racing with
The moon,
Elated from the morning meditation, when you see from seemingly out of nowhere,
Two deer
Prancing down the road towards
YOU.

You
Are in the center and the
Two deer,
If they continued along in the way they were running, would pass along side you at
the speed of deer, as you would glide through their
Gait.

But they STOP, a few meters before they reach you, and you stop too.
You stand face to face with them, the moon high above to your left, their right.

After some moments of silence, you want to say something, to greet them and this
moment,
So you scream
A true meditative
Ahhhhhhhhhhhhhhhh.
The deer remain still, listening.

Just as you watch the sound trailing off into silence, the deer
Gracefully (as all deer are)
Exit
Left
Into
The woods.

Did we talk about drinks,
or are we sticking
to water?
Asked the waitress who had just
taken our order.

Photo by Joanne G. Yoshida

Contributors

OLGA ABELLA teaches creative writing and literature at Eastern Illinois University and has published poems in *black dirt, CALYX, Urban Spaghetti, Natural Bridge, The MacGuffin, poetrybay.com, poetpourri, Long Island Quarterly, Ginosko, Kalliope,* and others. She is editor of the literary journal *Bluestem* (formerly *Karamu*).

MARCI AMELUXEN'S poems have appeared in *The Comstock Review, Waccamaw, Passager, Off Channel, Hospital Drive, The Dirty Napkin, Literary Mama.* She received 3rd Prize in the 2005 Hackney Literary Awards. Her chapbook manuscript *The Daughter Speaks*, of which "My Mother Visits Frida Kahlo" is an excerpt, was awarded Honorable Mention in the Clockwise Chapbook Competition 2010 of Tebot Bach press, and was a semifinalist in the Goldline Press Chapbook Competition, 2010. She works as a pediatric Occupational Therapist, and lives on an island in Puget Sound with her husband and two children.

ROBYN ART is the author of *The Stunt Double In Winter* (Dusie Press) and the text-visual collaboration with artists Robin Barcus Slonina, *Dear American Love Child, Yours, The Beautiful Undead* (forthcoming from dancing girl press.) Her recent work appears in *The Denver Quarterly, 42opus*, and *Blueline.* She lives in Maplewood, NJ, with her husband and young daughters, and teaches at New Jersey City University.

Twenty-five-year-old A.M. BAKER lives in Orlando, FL where she can be found writing in her garage amongst geckos when not chasing her rambunctious pre-schooler. Her fiction can be found in *3:AM Magazine* and *Opium Magazine*; her nonfiction can be found in various places as well. In June she will receive her MFA in Creative Writing from Goddard College.

KELLY BARGABOS currently resides in Syracuse, New York. She enjoys writing about the things that move her and hopes they move you too. She is an active member of the Downtown Writer's Center and finds excellent instruction there to hone her craft.

MARGO BERDESHEVSKY'S poetry collection, *But A Passage In Wilderness,* was published by Sheep Meadow Press, who will also publish her newest book of poetry, *Between Soul and Stone* (forthcoming in fall 2011). Her *Beautiful Soon Enough* (University of Alabama Press, 2009) her collection of cutting edge and illustrated short stories, received FC2's American Book Review/ Ronald Sukenick Award for Innovative Fiction. Other honors include the Poetry Society of America›s Robert H. Winner Award, six Pushcart Prize nominations, two Pushcart "Special Mention citations" for works in *AGNI, Pleiades, Kenyon Review, New Letters, Poetry International, Southern Review, Chelsea, Kalliope, Poetry Daily.* A cross-genre novel, *Vagrant* is next, from Red Hen Press. She currently lives in Paris. http://www.redroom.com/author/margo-berdeshevsky, http://margoberdeshevsky.blogspot.com.

CAROL BERG has poems forthcoming or in *Artifice, Fifth Wednesday Journal, Pebble Lake Review, blossombones, qarrtsiluni, Melusine,* and elsewhere. Her chapbook, *Ophelia Unraveling,* is forthcoming from dancing girl press. She has an MFA from Stonecoast. http://carolbergpoetry.com/wordpress/.

Born in Trinidad and raised in Queens, New York, CHERYL BOYCE-TAYLOR is a poet, teaching artist and mother, and the author of three collections of poetry, *Raw Air, Night When Moon Follows* and *Convincing the Body.* Her work was recently published in four new anthologies: *Caribbean Erotic, So Much Things to Say: 100 Calabash Poets, Encyclopedia Vol. 11 F-K, and For the Crowns of Your Heads: Poems for Haiti.* Boyce-Taylor earned her MFA in Poetry from Stonecoast, University of Southern Maine, and is currently working on a new manuscript titled *Wild Sorrel.* She dedicates these poems to her late mother, Eugenia Boyce, who read poems to her at bedtime.

TAMMY BRADSHAW is a teacher, writer, photographer, and first-time mom who lives in Philadelphia, PA. Her work has recently been published in *Shaking Like a Mountain*, *491 Magazine*, *Phillyist*, and *WHYY's Radio Times*. She has a passion for life's tiny details and the beauty that can be captured with words and in snapshots. She uses art and writing to maintain ongoing conversations with the world. http://tammybradshawphoto.blogspot.com/.

SARAH WERTHAN BUTTENWIESER is a graduate of Hampshire College and the MFA for Writers Program at Warren Wilson College. A former reproductive rights organizer/educator, she writes about women, motherhood, the arts & more. Her work has appeared on *Literary Mama, Mamazine, & Mothers Movement Online*, in *Brain Child, Family Fun* and *Ars Medica*, amongst others & in anthologies, most recently *The Maternal is Political* (Seal Press) edited by Shari MacDonald Strong. She lives in Northampton, Massachusetts, with her husband, four children & zero pets. Her blog, Standing in the Shadows, is at http://www.valleyadvocate.com/blogs/standingintheshadows.

ROSALIE CALABRESE lives and works in New York City, where she is a management consultant for the arts. Her poems have appeared in many publications, ranging from *And Then* to *Cosmopolitan, Jewish Currents* to *Poetry New Zealand* as well as newspapers, anthologies, and on the Web. In addition to poetry, she writes short stories and books and lyrics for musicals.

SHARON CAMPBELL is mom to two school-age boys and lives in Davis, CA. She studied at St. John's College in Santa Fe, and in the Committee on Social Thought at the University of Chicago. She won the 2010 Jack Kerouac Poetry Prize and is a Pushcart nominee.

CARLA CARLSON is a poet/writer, wife and mother, living in Pelham Manor, New York. Her present themes emerge from a mindful review of her first twenty-five years with her husband, and raising their five children in Westchester. She studies at the Writing Center at Sarah Lawrence College, and the Hudson Valley Writers Center, in Sleepy Hollow, NY.

PATRICIA CARRAGON is a New York City writer and poet. Her work can be found online and in anthologies. She hosts the Brooklyn-based Brownstone Poets and is the editor of its annual anthology. She is the author of *Journey to the Center of My Mind* (Rogue Scholars Press, 2005). Her latest book is *Urban Haiku and More* (Fierce Grace Press, 2010). She is a member of Brevitas, a group dedicated to short poems.

LIANE KUPFERBERG CARTER'S work has appeared in numerous publications, including the *New York Times* Motherlode, the *Huffington Post, Babble, Skirt!, Literary Mama, Parents, Memoir(and), Errant Parent, Mr. Beller's Neighborhood* and *Brevity*. She is a 2009 winner of the *Memoir Journal* Prize for Memoir in Prose, and a *Glimmer Train* finalist in poetry. This work is excerpted from a memoir in progress, *Love is Like This: A Family Grows Up with Autism*. She blogs at http://www.huffingtonpost.com/liane-kupferberg-carter.

SARAH CAVALLARO is a writer who just finished a screenplay "Bitter Sweet," which is about an artist who created a chocolate Jesus. She is a film producer who started Emerald Films, which produces art installations, commercials, and documentaries.

MRB CHELKO is a recent graduate of The University of New Hampshire's MFA program and Assistant Editor of the unbound journal, *Tuesday; An Art Project*. She has poems in current or forthcoming issues of *AGNI Online, Bateau, Forklift, Ohio, The Laurel Review, Sixth Finch,* and *Washington Square* among others. Chelko has two chapbooks: *The World after Czeslaw Milosz* (Dream Horse Press, 2011), which won the 2010 Dream Horse Press National Chapbook Prize, and *What to Tell the Sleeping Babies* (sunnyoutside, 2010). She lives in Central Harlem with her husband, Nick, and dog, Chuck. www.pw.org/content/mrb_chelko.

FLOYD CHEUNG'S poetry has appeared in the *Naugatuck River Review*, the *New Verse News*, the *Apple Valley Review*, and other journals. He teaches at Smith College in Northampton, Massachusetts.

FAY CHIANG is a poet and visual artist who believes culture is a spiritual and psychological weapon used for the empowerment of people and communities. Working at Project Reach (www.projectreach.org), a youth center for young people at risk in Chinatown/Lower East Side, she is also a member of Zero Capital, a collective of artists (www.zerocapital.net); the Orchard Street Advocacy and Wellness Center, which supports people affected by HIV/AIDS, cancer and other chronic illnesses. Battling her 8th bout of breast cancer, she is completing *Chinatown*, a book-length poem and a memoir. *Seven Continents 9 Lives*, new and selected work, was recently released by Bowery Books.

HEATHER LYNNE DAVIS is the author of *The Lost Tribe of Us*, which won the 2007 Main Street Rag Poetry Book Award. Her poems have appeared in *Cream City Review, Gargoyle, Poet Lore, Puerto del Sol*, and *Sonora Review*, among other journals. With her husband, the poet José Padua, she writes the blog Shenandoah Breakdown at http://shenandoahbreakdown.wordpress.com.

NICELLE DAVIS lives in Southern California with her son J.J. Her poems have appeared or are forthcoming in *Broadsided, Front Range, FuseLit, Moulin Review, ML Press, The New York Quarterly, Offending Adam, Picture Postcard Press, SLAB Magazine, Superficial Flesh, Transcurrent Literary Journal, Two Review*, and others. She'd like to acknowledge her poetry family at the University of California, Riverside and Antelope Valley Community College. She runs a free online poetry workshop at The Bees' Knees Blog, http://nicelledavis.wordpress.com/.

HOLLY DAY is a journalism instructor living in Minneapolis, Minnesota, with her husband and two children. Her most recent nonfiction books are *Music Theory for Dummies, Music Composition for Dummies*, and *Guitar All-in-One for Dummies*. Her poetry and fiction has most recently appeared in *Willow Review, The Blotter*, and *Pinyon*.

SANDRA DE HELEN lives and writes in Portland, Oregon where she belongs to Penplay. De Helen is a proud member of the Dramatists Guild and International Centre for Women Playwrights. See more of her poetry on her Facebook page and on her blog http://dehelensbits.blogspot.com/. Her other works are at www.SandradeHelen.com.

WENDY LEVINE DEVITO lives in Hartsdale, New York with her husband and two children. Her poems have appeared in *The Mom Egg, Literary Mama, The Ampersand Review* and *Poetica*. She is completing her first chapbook, *A Place in the Center*. She teaches English.

CAROL DORF'S poems have appeared in *In Posse Review, Moira, A Cappella Zoo, Naugatuck River Review, Feminist Studies, Fringe, The Midway, Poemeleon, Runes, 13th Moon*, and have been anthologized in *Not a Muse, Boomer Girls*, and elsewhere. She is the poetry editor of *Talking Writing*, and her reviews appear in *New Pages*. Having taught in a variety of venues (including arts' centers and at a science museum), she currently teaches math at Berkeley High School. Being the mother of a 14-year-old is teaching her to negotiate new boundaries.

JACQUELINE DOYLE'S flash fiction and memoir have appeared in *elimae, flashquake, blossombones, onepagestories, DOGZPLOT, Staccato Fiction, Glossolalia, LITnIMAGE* and a number of other online journals. She also has creative nonfiction published and forthcoming in *SNReview, River Poets Journal, Pear Noir!, Women's Studies* and elsewhere. She lives in the San Francisco Bay Area, where she teaches at California State University, East Bay.

IRIS JAMAHL DUNKLE teaches literature and writing at Clarion University in Pennsylvania. Her chapbook *Inheritance* was published by Finishing Line (2010). Her poetry, creative nonfiction and scholarly articles have appeared in numerous publications including: *Fence, LinQ, Boxcar Poetry Review, Cleveland in Prose and Poetry, Eaden Water's Press Home Anthology* and *The Squaw Valley Writers Review.*

JENNIFER EDWARDS writes for the Huffington Post, publishing pieces on dance, health, and politics. She and her work as a stress management teacher have been featured in the *New York Times* and Martha Stewart's *Whole Living Magazine.* As the founder of JenEd Productions, Jennifer creates content and programing for organizations including: the American Heart Association, NYU Tisch School of the Arts, Dance / NYC, and The Joyful Heart Foundation. For more information, visit www.jened.com.

A. KAY EMMERT is a native Oklahoman who received her MFA from Georgia College where she taught composition and creative writing. While at Georgia College she also served as associate editor on the *Arts & Letters* staff and coordinated a WITS program which introduces writing to 7th graders of Bill Gates funded school, Early College. Among the many landscapes of the US, she has had the pleasure of living among the lakes of Minnesota, the Arkansas Ozarks, and the borderlands of New Mexico and she has loved them all. Her poems have previously appeared in *Kestrel.*

JANN EVERARD is a writer-mom married to a mountaineer/marathon runner with two teenaged sons. She was educated (in part) in an American school in Europe but now calls Toronto, Canada home. Her essays and short fiction have been published most recently in *Room, The Nashwaak Review, The Los Angeles Review* and *Existere,* as well as in several anthologies, newspapers and online. She is currently working on a novel for middle-grade readers set in the Himalayas.

ELEANOR GAFFNEY is a teacher and a poet living in Nyack, NY. She has a MAW from Manhattanville College and has been published by *The Westchester Review* and *Alimentum.* Eleanor teaches English to recent immigrants, both adults and teens. She has two adult sons and is still learning how to parent.

MARIE GAUTHIER is the author of a chapbook, *Hunger All Inside* (Finishing Line Press, 2009). Recent poems can be read in *The MacGuffin, Cave Wall, Hunger Mountain,* and elsewhere, and she won a 2008 Dorothy Sargent Rosenberg Poetry Prize. She lives with her husband and two young sons in Shelburne Falls, MA where she works for Tupelo Press and co-curates the Collected Poets Series. http://mariegauthier.wordpress.com.

NANCY GERBER is the author of "My Mother's Keeper," a chronicle of her mother's struggle with Alzheimer's published by The Feral Press.

JANLORI GOLDMAN received an MFA in poetry from Sarah Lawrence College. Her poems have been published, or are forthcoming, in *Mudlark, The Cortland Review, The Mom Egg, Calyx, Connotations Press, The Sow's Ear,* and, *For the Crowns of Their Heads: Poems for Haiti.* She teaches health and human rights at Columbia University, and lives in New York City with her teenage daughter and her sweetheart.

BRIONY GYLGAYTON has won multiple awards for her writing, including placing in the Ina Coolbrith Memorial Poetry Prize and the Pamela Maus Contests for Creative Writing. *Louder Walls,* her manuscript of poetry about psychological disorders, was recently awarded the Elliot Gilbert Memorial Prize. Briony works as the producer of the Davis Poetry Night Reading Series. More of her work is available on her website, www.BrionyGylgayton.com.

HEATHER HALDEMAN began writing professionally eleven years ago. Her work has been published in *The Christian Science Monitor, Chicken Soup for the Soul, The Mom Egg, From Freckles to Wrinkles* and *Grandmother Earth.* She has received several online journal awards for her essays. Heather and her husband, Hank, live in Pasadena, California and have three grown children.

MARYANNE HANNAN has published work in numerous print and online journals, including *Magma, Naugatuck River Review, Pebble Lake Review, Stand, Umbrella*, and *upstreet*. A Contributing Editor at *Cerise Press: A Journal of Literature, Arts and Culture*, she is a mother and grandmother.

PAULETTA HANSEL is the author of three collections of poetry, *Divining, First Person* and *The Lives We Live in Houses*, to be published by Wind Publications in Fall 2011. Her poetry is featured in journals and anthologies including *ABZ Jorunal, Appalachian Journal, Penwood Review, A Gathering at the Forks; Motif: Come What May*, and *Listen Here: Women Writing in Appalachia*. A native of Kentucky's Appalachian Mountains, Pauletta is Co-Director of Grailville Retreat and Program Center in Loveland Ohio, and holds an MFA from Queens University.

LOIS MARIE HARROD'S eleventh book, *Brief Term, (poems of teachers, students and teaching)* has just been published by Black Buzzard Press. Her *Cosmogony* won the 2010 Flyway Hazel Lipa Chapbook contest (Iowa State University) and her *Furniture* won the 2008 Grayson Press Poetry Prize. She teaches Creative Writing and supervises student teachers part-time at The College of New Jersey. Visit her website www.loismarieharrod.com.

LOUISA HOWEROW'S poems have appeared in British, Canadian, and American publications, such as *Bateau, Passager, Sojourn*, and *The Yalobusha Review.*. Her poetry has been nominated for the Canadian National Magazine Award.

WYNNE HUDDLESTON is a mother, grandmother, music teacher, and a board member of the Mississippi Writers Guild. Winner of the 2010 *Grandmother Earth* Environmental Poetry Contest, Ms. Huddleston has been, or will be, published in *Camroc Press Review, Raven Chronicles, Birmingham Arts Journal, THEMA, The Stray Branch, Enchanted Conversation, Gemini Magazine, Emerald Tales, The Shine Journal* and elsewhere. http://wynnehuddleston.wordpress.com/.

American SUZANNE KAMATA is the author of the novel *Losing Kei* (Leapfrog Press, 2008) and a short story collection, *The Beautiful One Has Come* (Wyatt-Mackenzie Publishing, 2011). She is also the editor of three anthologies including *Love You to Pieces: Creative Writers on Raising a Child with Special Needs* (Beacon Press, May 2008). She currently lives in Japan with her Japanese husband and bicultural twins. Her website is http://www.suzannekamata.com.

KELLI STEVENS KANE'S poetry appears in numerous journals including *Word Riot, Kweli Journal*, and *Mythium Literary Journal*. She's the recipient of a 2011 Flight School Fellowship, an alum of the VONA and Hurston/Wright poetry workshops, the editor of Planet Saturday Comics, and the author of an oral history manuscript about Pittsburgh's Hill District. She has performed nationally. For more information visit www.planetsaturday.com/kelli/.

DONNA KATZIN is Executive Director of Shared Interest, a non-profit investment fund that advances equitable development in South Africa's communities of color. Her poetry is informed by he work, her family and struggles for social justice.

CHERYL KEELER opened and manages the branch library in the Virginia town where she lives with her husband and where she is taken on brisk morning walks by her rescued Jack Russell. She has published several short stories for children in *Highlights* and *Jack and Jill*, and poems in *5AM, The Dirty Napkin* (online) and *International Psychoanalysis* (online).

CHRISTOPHER KULAKOWSKI is in his third year at the University of Pittsburgh, pursuing the Writing Poetry major. He is the lyricist and singer for a local Pittsburgh band called Capax Infiniti. Unsure of his career path, he plans to just keep writing, singing, and helping others to find some sort of contentment. You can find some of his more lyrical work at www.facebook.com/capaxinfiniti.

KRISTIN LAUREL completed a two-year apprenticeship in poetry at The Loft Literary Center this year. She is a mother of three, employed as a nurse. She has recently been published or has work forthcoming in, *The Battered Suitcase, Calyx, Grey Sparrow Journal, Hospital Drive, Mainstreet Rag, Naugatuck River Review, Prose Poem Project, The Talking Stick,* and other journals. She has a chapbook, *You Might Feel a Little Poke*, and a full length book of poetry, *Giving Them All Away*, that are in the final stages of revision.

After thirty years as a psychotherapist, CAROLINE A. LEBLANC retired to create art and lead creativity groups. Her poetry has been published in the US and abroad. Much of her work focuses on her Franco-American heritage, and her life as an Army Nurse, wife, and mother. In May 2011, she will complete her MFA in Creative Writing at Spalding University.

JAN HELLER LEVI, who teaches at Hunter College in New York, is the author of *Once I Gazed at You in Wonder* and *Skyspeak*, both from Louisiana State University Press. She's also the editor of *A Muriel Rukeyser Reader,* co-editor with Sara Miles of *Directed by Desire: The Collected Poems of June Jordan,* and is an honorary advisor for the Language of Conservation, a Poet's House program dedicated to deepening public awareness of environmental issues through poetry.

ELSA MANDELBAUM writes poetry and prose and creates mixed media paintings. Her work has been presented at Antioch University and Richard Hugo House, and published in *Rewrite.* Her current work explores the individual journey of healing. She lives with her husband in Seattle. Her work can be found at www.elsamandelbaum.com.

KATIE MANNING lives with her husband in Louisiana, where she is a doctoral fellow in English at UL-Lafayette, Editor-in-Chief of *Rougarou*, and a daily visitor to the nearby swamp. Her poems have been published in *New Letters, PANK, The Pedestal Magazine, Poet Lore*, and *So to Speak,* among other journals and anthologies. http://english.louisiana.edu/rougarou/.

BLUEBERRY ELIZABETH MORNINGSNOW is a poet, teacher, and the mother of Finnegan (he is 2 and a half). She received her MFA in poetry from the Iowa Writers' Workshop. She has poems published most recently in *notnostrums* and *Propeller.* She believes in the imagination.

SUSAN MORSE writes many poems that explore women's lives, especially mother/daughter relationships. She was born and raised in California, but moved to rural Maine in the 1980's. Most of her family lives on the West Coast. Both of her daughters attended college in California and decided to remain there after graduation. These poems help preserve connection with family. Other poems have been published in *The Cream City Review* and *The Aurorean.*

Brooklyn-based freelance writer and editor RACHAEL LYNN NEVINS teaches fiction and poetry writing online for the Writers Studio. She writes about making her way toward work-life balance in a family of artists at The Variegated Life (thevariegatedlife.com) and has work forthcoming in *RATTLE.*

ASHLEY NISSLER lives in Hillsborough, North Carolina with her husband and two daughters. Her work has appeared in/at *Cricket, Ladybug, Strange Horizons, Tar River Poetry, Literary Mama, poemeleon, The Black Boot* and *Vestal Review.*

ELIANA OSBORN lives in the desert southwest, trying to raise a husband and two young sons. She has been published in *Budget Travel, Diabetes Health, Literary Mama,* and various parenting magazines. She dreams of a day when no one will bother her in the bathroom. She blogs at Slightly Hyperbolic about the vagaries of daily life.

CARL PALMER, president of the Tacoma Writers Club, nominee for three Pushcart Prizes and Micro Award, from Old Mill Road in Ridgeway, VA, now lives in University Place, WA.

ANIKA PARIS is a platinum selling songwriter, and Abe Oleman Scholarship at the Songwriters Hall of Fame recipient. Her songs are featured in major motion pictures and soundtracks. Currently she and writing partner Dean Landon are composing for the musical opera *Temple of the Souls* and her first book Making Your Mark in Music (Hal Leonard) is in stores September 2011. Her poems have appeared in: *Chance of a Ghost, In the Black In the Red* (Helicon Nine), *Poets Without Borders*, (Gival Press), *Soft Blow Poetry, All in the Family*, (Spillway #15) and more.

PUMA PERL is a NYC based poet/writer/performance artist/producer. Her work has been widely published, and she is the author of *Belinda and Her Friends* and *knuckle tattoos*. She performs her work in many venues, in and out of New York City, and is a founding member of DDAY Productions, which showcases female poets and performance artists monthly, at the Yippie Museum Café, NYC. More information on blog, http://pumaperl.blogspot.com/

TESS PFEIFER is a librarian in Western Massachusetts and mother to two sons. Her poems have appeared in *Verse, The Massachusetts Review*, and *Margie*, as well as other journals. Her manuscript has been a finalist in the Snowbound Chapbook and the Intuit House Competition from *Margie*. She is a recipient of a Massachusetts Artist Grant in Poetry and was a judge for the 2010 Massachusetts Book Awards.

BARBARA ROCKMAN teaches poetry at Santa Fe Community College and in private workshops in Santa Fe, NM Her poems have appeared or are forthcoming in *Bellingham Review, Calyx, Cimarron Review, Louisville Review, Spoon River Poetry Review* and *Terrain.org*. She is editor of the anthology, *Women Becoming Poems (*Cinabar Press). A graduate of the MFA in Writing Program at Vermont College of Fine Arts, her collection, *Sting and Nest*, has recently been published by Sunstone Press.

KRISTIN ROEDELL graduated from Whitman College (B.A. English 1984) and the University of Washington Law School (J.D. 1987). Her poetry has appeared in *Switched on Gutenberg, Ginosko, Flutter, Damselflypress, Chantarelle's Notebook, Eclectica, Quill* and *Parchment* (featured poet January 2010) *Open Minds Quarterly, Ekphrasis, The Fertile Source, City Arts, Breath and Shadow, Pilgrimage, Cliterature, Soundings Review, Metromania* and *Four and Twenty*. Other poems will appear in *Chest, Voice Catcher Anthology,* and *Touch: a Journal of Healing* (Editor's Choice, September 2010). Her chapbook *Seeing in the Dark* was published in 2009 by Tomato Can Press.

ROSALY DEMAIOS ROFFMAN is Professor Emeritus at Indiana University of Penna. She is the co-editor of *Life on the Line* and author of *Going to Bed Whole, Tottering Palaces, The Approximate Message* and *In the Fall of A Sparrow*, and forthcoming from Tebot Bach Press, *I Want to Thank My Eyes*. Roffman has collaborated with composers and dance/theater companies and has been published in journals and anthologies including *Macguffin, Zone 3, Centennial Review, Pittsburgh Quarterly, Sing Heavenly Muse*, and in the anthologies *Along These Rivers, Only The Sea Keeps*, and *Come Together: Imagine Peace*. The recipient of a Distinguished Faculty Award in the Arts in Pa., and of National Endowment Grants, she is member and facilitator of the Squirrel Hill Poetry Workshop in Pittsburgh.

CHANELL RUTH, MFA, serving Poetry Editor of *Warpland Literary Journal*, assisted with *Dream of a Word*. Her poems have been appeared in *The Louisiana English Journal, Fingernails Across the Chalkboard, Reverie, Spaces Between Us, The Tidal Basin* and curated in *The Citizen's Picnic: Lynching in America from 1865 to Present* in 2008. Chanell teaches English Composition, and is a Hurston/Wright alum.

LEE SCHWARTZ lives with her husband in an empty nest in Greenwich Village. She has recently written a chapbook about raising a gay daughter, entitled *Invisible Ink*. Through this poetic journey Lee has become outed and is an active supporter of LGBTQ issues and forums.

PETER SEIDMAN was born in Chicago, and was educated in the Heartland as well as on both coasts. He retired several years ago from life as a teacher, R&D program manager, and editor. Peter has been published among other sources in *Gertrude 13, River Poets Journal, Presence, Wild Goose Poetry Review, The green tricycle*, as well as in *Beyond Forgetting: Poetry and Prose about Alzheimer's Disease*. He lives in Berkeley, California.

JUDITH SKILLMAN is the author of twelve full-length collections of poetry. She is the recipient of grants from Washington State Arts Commission, Academy of American Poets, and other organizations. Her poems have appeared in *Midwest Quarterly, The Iowa Review, Journal of the American Medical Association (JAMA), New Poets of the American West,* and other journals and anthologies. Skillman teaches on occasion for the Richard Hugo House. A collection about the seven deadly sins titled *The White Cypress* will be published by Cervéna Barva Press in 2011. www.judithskillman.com.

DANIELLE TAANA SMITH is an associate professor of sociology at Rochester Institute of Technology. Her essays, articles and poetry have appeared in various scholarly and literary journals. She is also the co-editor of *Cultures of Fear: A Critical Reader*, an interdisciplinary volume with essays by leading scholars that investigate the everyday regimes of fear in a global context.

GOLDA SOLOMON, poet, performer hosts Po'Jazz at The Cornelia Street Café, Greenwich Village, NYC and takes her JazzHag tour on the road with outstanding musicians. Be on the lookout for her new collection, *Medicine Woman of Jazz*, published by World Audience. Golda continues to facilitate, ArtSpeak: From Page To Performance, ekphrastic writing workshops partially funded by Poets & Writers at Blue Door Gallery, Yonkers, NY where she is poet-in-residence. Contact Solomon at gs@goldajazz.com and check out her activities through her website: www.jazzjaunts.com.

LYDIA SUAREZ's stories and poems have appeared in publications including *Prism Review, Pearl* and the Warren Adler Short Story Anthology. Most recently, a collection of stories was selected as a finalist in the Grace Notes Competition and an unpublished novel was chosen as a semifinalist for the Elixir Press Fiction Award. By profession she is a psychologist who in her spare time watches telenovelas with improbable plots with her mother.

JUDY SWANN has been published in *Lilliput, Literary Bohemian, Thema, Verse Wisconsin, Short, Fast, & Deadly*, and other venues, both print and online. She is a mother, a foster mother, a legal guardian, and a care provider.

CHRISTINA THOMPSON is the editor of Harvard Review and the author of the memoir, *Come on Shore and We Will Kill and Eat You All* (Bloomsbury, 2008), which was shortlisted for the 2010 William Saroyan International Prize for Writing and the 2009 New South Wales Premier's Literary Award. She is currently at work on a book about the ancient voyagers of the Pacific titled *The Wonder Story of the World.* www.comeonshore.com www.seapeople.wordpress.com.

TINA TRASTER is the author of *Burb Appeal: The Collection*, a collection of her New York Post Burb Appeal column. Traster also writes The Great Divide blog for The Huffington Post. Her work has appeared in newspapers, magazines, literary journals and on NPR. Her essays have been anthologized in *Living Lessons* and *Mammas and Pappas*. Traster lives in an old but renovated farmhouse with her husband, daughter, five rescued cats and six hens. www.tinatraster.com.

MEREDITH TREDE is a founding publisher of Toadlily Press. Her chapbook, *Out of the Book,* was in *Desire Path,* the inaugural volume of The Quartet Series. Some journals that have published her work are *Barrow Street, Blue Mesa Review, Gargoyle, The Paris Review* and *13th Moon.* She has also been awarded residency fellowships at Blue Mountain Center, Ragdale, Saltonstall, and the Virginia Center for the Creative Arts in Virginia and France.

ELSBETH WOFFORD TYLER struggles to find hope in the darkness through the medium of her work. She is the active, full-time mother of five children, ages 6 weeks to 9 years. She currently resides in North Georgia on the border between states, families, and realities.

CLAUDIA VAN GERVEN teaches writing in Boulder, Colorado. Her poems have been published in a number journals, including *Prairie Schooner* and *Calyx*. Her work has appeared in numerous anthologies and has been nominated for the Pushcart Prize. Her chapbook, *The Ends of Sunbonnet Sue,* won the Angel Fish Press Poetry Prize. Her most recent chapbook is *Amazing Grace*, (Green Fuse Poetic Arts, 2010).

WENDY VARDAMAN lives in Madison, Wisconsin and is the author of *Obstructed View* (Fireweed Press 2009). She works for The Young Shakespeare Players, a children's theater company, co-edits *Verse Wisconsin*, www.versewisconsin.org, has three children, and does not own a car. www.wendyvardaman.com

NANCY VONA graduated from the University of New Hampshire with an M.A. in Creative Writing in 1989. She has worked as a freelance writer, editor, and teacher of science writing. The birth of her first son Daniel renewed her interest in creative writing, and she self-published a chapbook of poetry and essays, *The Book of Daniel*, in 2005. She has poetry published in *Literary Mama, Rushlight*, and an upcoming issue of *Mothering*. She lives with her husband and two sons in Massachusetts.

JONATHAN WELLS is a poet and editor. His poems have been published or are forthcoming in *Hayden's Ferry, Nimrod , Poetry International, Alaska Quarterly Review*, and *The New Yorker*. He is also the editor of *Third Rail: An Anthology of Rock and Roll* (Simon & Schuster and MTV Books). A new book of poetry, *Train Dance*, is forthcoming from Four Way Books in October, 2011.

L.B. WILLIAMS is the author of the memoir, *Letters to Virginia Woolf*, published by Hamilton Books (June 2005), www.letterstovirginiawoolf.com. She also wrote *The Artist as Outsider in the Novels of Toni Morrison and Virginia Woolf* (Greenwood Press, 2000). Lisa's work has appeared in such publications as *The Mom Egg, The Women's Studies Quarterly, The Tusculum Review, The Virginia Woolf Miscellany*, and *For She is the Tree of Life: Grandmothers Through the Eyes of Women Writers*. She teaches writing and literature at Ramapo College of New Jersey.

RHONDA WOODWARD is a Hyla Brook Poet associated with the Frost Farm in Derry, New Hampshire. She lives with her husband and three children in Chester, NH, where she also teaches yoga and works as a special educator. Lindsay, her youngest, recently became a teenager.

JOANNE G. YOSHIDA is a visual artist and poet who lives in Oita, Japan with her husband and daughter. Her visual art has appeared most recently on the covers of *Incidental Music* and *Yomimono*, and her writing in *Things Japanese, Kyoto Journal, The Pennsylvania Gazette* and *The Mom Egg*. She chronicles her daily life and other projects on several blogs including aikawarazulifeinjapan.blogspot.com, tomarejgy.blogspot.com, and paintingsandworksonpaperjgy.blogspot.com.

Made in the USA
Charleston, SC
26 April 2011